Helion & Company Limited
26 Willow Road
Solihull
West Midlands
B91 1UE
England
Tel. 0121 705 3393
Fax 0121 711 4075
email: info@helion.co.uk
website: www.helion.co.uk
Twitter: @helionbooks
Visit our blog http://blog.helion.co.uk

Published by Helion & Company 2018

Designed and typeset by Farr out Publications, Wokingham, Berkshire
Cover designed by Paul Hewitt, Battlefield Design (www.battlefield-design.co.uk)
Printed by Henry Ling Limited, Dorchester, Dorset

ISBN 978-1-912174-95-9

British Library Cataloguing-in-Publication Data
A catalogue record for this book is available from the British Library

CONTENTS

Abbreviations

API	Accion Popular Independiente (Popular Independent Action)
CIA	Central Intelligence Agency, United States
CDP	Chile Declassification Project, Freedom of Information Act Reading Room, Department of State
C-in-C	Commander in chief
CODE	Confederation Democratica (Democratic Confederation)
CUT	Central Unica of Trabajadores (Unified Workers' Central)
DGLN	Departamento General de Liberacion Nacional (General National Liberation Department), Ministry of the Interior, Cuba
DGLN	Departamento General de Liberacion Nacional (General National Liberation Department), Ministry of the Interior, Cuba.
DIA	Defense Intelligence Agency, United States.
AK	Avtomat Kalashnikova (Kalashnikov assault rifle)
ELN	Ejercito de Liberacion Nacional, (National Liberation Army)
FF. AA	Fuerzas Armadas (Chilean Armed Forces)
FPMR	Frente Patriotico Manuel Rodriguez (Patriotic Front Manuel Rodriguez)
FRAP	Frente de Acción Popular (Popular Action Front)
ITT	International Telephone and Telegraph Corporation
GAP	Grupo de Amigos Personales (Group of Personal Friends)
GDR	German Democratic Republic
GEO	Grupos Especiales Operativos (operative special groups)
JCR	Junta Coordinadora Revolucionaria
MAPU	Movimiento de Acción Popular (Movement of Popular Unitary Action)
MIR	Movimiento de Izquierda Revolucionario (Movement of the Revolutionary Left)
PCCh	Partido Comunista de Chile (Chilean Communist Party)
PDC	Partido Democrata Cristiana (Christian Democratic Party)
PN	Partido Nacional (National Party)
PPD	Partido por Democracia (Party for Democracy)
PS	Partido Socialista (Socialist Party)
RPG	rocket-propelled grenade
STASI	Ministerium für Staatssicherheit (state security service of the German Democratic Republic)
UP	Unidad Popular (Popular Unity)
US$	United States Dollar
USSR	Union of Soviet Socialist Republics (or 'Soviet Union')

CHAPTER 1

INTRODUCTION

Of the many military coups that took place in the countries of Latin America, the coup in Chile of 11 September 1973 engraved itself most permanently on the collective memory. The images of the bombing of La Moneda Palace, of the despair on the face of Salvador Allende shortly before his suicide, of the defiant expression worn by Major-General Augusto Pinochet behind his dark glasses still make circles around the world and became the symbol of military brutality.

In the early 1970s, Chile was the most democratic country in the Spanish-speaking world — Latin America, Spain and Portugal included. The coup of 11 September 1973 was not only a classic pronunciamento in the descendants of those who punctuated the history of the South American continent: in the national context, it ended the presidency of Salvador Allende, a president who tried to establish socialism the peaceful way and by lawful means. Such ideas collided with those who maintained of the existing order.

Chilean society became divided between supporters and adversaries of the government, and every camp radicalised starting in 1972. The country was in the grip of ever more violent political crises in which the Right, welded by anticommunism and its rejection of any form of socialism, confronted the Left that radicalised as soon as it understood that the respect for institutional logic hindered revolutionary process.

At least initially, the Chilean armed forces played the referee's role in this conflict. In spite of the doctrine of national security instilled across the continent by means of the American military, the constitutionalism of the Chilean army remained strong until 1970. Subsequently it disappeared amid exacerbating dynamics. Eventually, political crisis prompted it into a coup nominally led by Pinochet.

This coup took place within an international context too – that of the Cold War. The revolutionary contents of Allende's politics transgressed the limits tolerated by the United States of America (USA) within the Western hemisphere – similar to the threats the former Union of the Soviet Socialist Republics (USSR, also Soviet Union) considered perceptible within its sphere of influence. Powers in Washington could not tolerate a 'second Cuba', and thus could not tolerate socialism in Chile – if for no other reason than because a country in which an alliance between communists and socialists would respect democratic practices, political pluralism and the rights of its citizens could become a precedent for similar developments in countries like France or Italy. The Chilean experience thus had a world-wide echo, and its tragic end marked the end of the dream of the democratic socialist alternative to the authoritarian, Soviet-style communism.

Finally, 11 September 1973 was a military operation which delivered the nail in the coffin of the Chilean democracy, installed a violent dictatorship, and opened an entire epoch of 'dirty little wars' in Latin America. Not only in Chile, but elsewhere around Latin America too, the famous sentence by Carl von Clausewitz according to which 'war is continuation of politics by other means' seemed to be right.

Early History of Chile

The Portuguese explorer Ferdinand Magellan was the first European to visit present-day Chile, landing on the island of Chiloé in 1520 – after having crossed the strait that subsequently received his name. The region was then named *Tchili* after the native word for snow. The natives in question used to inhabit the entire area south of the Rapel River and were named the Mapuches: they had a fearsome reputation as skilled warriors. On the contrary, the tribes further north were subjected to the Incas of Peru, starting in 15th Century.

In 1525, the Spanish conquistador Francisco Pizarro and one of his captains, Diego de Almagro, launched the conquest of the area south of Cuzco. After three years of bloody adventures, the expedition found no gold and only encountered fierce resistance by the Mapuches – the only great native tribe to fight against invaders.

Pedro de Valdivia led a second expedition into southern Chile in 1540. Despite fierce resistance from the Mapuches, he succeeded in establishing several colonies, including Santiago de la Nueva Estremadura in 1541, Concepción in 1550, and Valdivia in 1552. In 1554, the Mapuches launched a major uprising, massacring Valdivia and many of his companions and devastating all cities except Concepción and La Serena.[1] The fighting continued intermittently during and after the period of colonization undertaken by Spain and ceased only in the late 19th Century.

In 1557, Spain, through a governor, took possession of the Chilean territory. Within this colonial empire, Chile was first a dependency of the viceroyalty of Peru, before having its own government led by a governor and a royal court. The development of the country was slow, particularly due to the absence of gold and silver mines to attract the Spaniards. Chile was also far from the great Peruvian colonization centres and difficult to access. Agriculture in the central valley was the main activity, allowing Chile to supply food products to Peru.[2]

The first nationalist ideas proclaiming Chilean independence emerged in the 18th Century, when two major movements appeared: the 'realists' and the 'patriots'. Upon their uprising, they officially announced the dismissal of the colonial governor, a take-over by an assembly of seven persons, and breaking all political ties with Spain in 1810. The insurgency brought most of the country under its control and thus realized Chilean independence: on 4 July 1811, the 1st National Congress elected a revolutionary junta lead by Bernardo O'Higgins as a new government.

Nevertheless, Spain re-conquered the country in a large campaign launched from Peru, from 1814 until 1817. Although defeated at Rancagua in October 1814, Chileans subsequently benefitted from support from Argentina, where Jose de San Martín deployed his army into an attack. On 12 February 1817, he defeated the Spanish army in the battle of Chacabuco, ending colonial rule in northern Chile. Refusing to take over, San Martín then designated O'Higgins a Supreme Dictator.

A year later, on 12 February 1818, Chile proclaimed its independence again. Even then, Spain retained control of most of the South until the battle of Maipú, in 1818, and its last troops were expelled from the country only in 1826.[3]

Meanwhile, O'Higgins was forced to resign in 1823, amid popular protest. The republic, established by the virtue of a liberal Constitution, was proclaimed at the instigation of Ramón Freire. Rivalries between numerous political parties sowed anarchy until 1830, when General Joaquin Prieto – head of the conservatives – fomented a revolt that allowed him to take power.[4] In 1831, Prieto became president, but the actual strongman in his government was Diego Portales, who occupied several ministries. A new Constitution – granting wide powers to the executive – was adopted in 1833.[5] Several times (in 1835, 1851 and 1859) the liberals failed in their attempts to overthrow the conservatives.

Under the conservative government, Chile's foreign policy was marked by a series of unresolved conflicts with neighbours. The first of these were with Peru and Bolivia in 1839, and culminated in the Battle of Yungay. The second was with Argentina in 1843-1881: several times it degenerated into open war, but was ended with the Tierra del Fuego Boundary Treaty. Subsequently, Chile launched exploitation of rich nitrate deposits in the Atacama Desert.

Rejecting Bolivia's pretensions to this territory, in February 1879, the Chilean army invaded the Bolivian port of Antofagasta. Two months later, Peru, an ally of Bolivia, declared war on Chile. Victorious in this 'Pacific War' of 1883, Chile considerably enlarged its territory, annexing the Bolivian province of Antofagasta and the Peruvian province of Tarapacá, and forcing Peru to cede Tacna.

In 1891, a close alliance between the political forces and the Catholic clergy revolted against the government of President José Manuel Balmaceda, leader of the Liberal Party. Under the command of Captain Jorge Montt, a naval officer, the rebels seized the Chilean fleet and the rich northern provinces. In August, they defeated the loyalist military near Valparaíso and captured this city, followed by Santiago. The fall of the capital marked the end of this civil war that left more than 10,000 killed and caused significant material damage before Balmaceda committed suicide in September 1891.[6] One of the consequences of this conflict was the orientation of the government towards a parliamentary system, granting more powers to Congress. Shortly thereafter, Montt became president, signalling a long period of peace and reconstruction.

A Country between Mountains and Ocean

On a map, Chile looks like a long ribbon, reaching from the middle of South America's west coast straight down to the southern tip of the continent, from the Peru to the Cape Horn, the southernmost points in the Americas, where the Pacific and Atlantic oceans turbulently meet. From north to south, Chile extends 4,270 km (2,653 mi), and yet it only averages 177 km (110 mi) east to west between the Pacific Ocean and the Andean Mountains.

Natural borders isolate Chile from its neighbours: it is separated from Argentina by the Cordillera of the Andes, Bolivia and Peru by the Atacama desert. The country is mainly composed of a zone of plains framed by two mountain ranges: the Andean, which marks the natural border with Bolivia and Argentina, and peaks in Ojos del Salado (6,893 meters); and the Cordillera, on the western coast, which peaks at about 2,000 meters.

Between the Cordillera of the Coast and the Pacific there is a series of coastal plains. The arid Atacama Desert in northern Chile contains great mineral wealth, principally copper. Settlement in this arid region is tied with the exploitation of minerals in the interior. A string of coastal cities, such as Iquique, Antofagasta, and Arica, emerged as export centres for nitrates, borax, and copper, and serve as administrative and trading centres. The only city of significance in the interior of the Norte Grande is Calama near the Chuquicamata copper mine.

Towards the south, the relatively small coastal plain dominates in terms of population and agricultural resources. It's the cultural and political centre allowing emergence of several bigger cities and ports. The centrepiece is Santiago de Chile, which grew into the country's major metropolis. Seventy miles (112km) west of Santiago is the port city of Valparaíso and the neighbouring resort city of Viña del Mar, which form the second largest population centre. In the Central Valley, south of the Santiago basin, there is a series of secondary cities, the development of which has been tied to the agricultural success of central Chile. On the coast of the southern Central Nucleus there is Concepción and its port city of Talcahuano. In the south of the Central Nucleus, Osorno and Puerto Montt are other regional centres, situated close to the Piedmont lakes and the snow-caped volcanoes.

Patagonia in Chile extends from the latitude of the 41st parallel south to the southern tip of the country. During the last ice age,

Stretching for almost 4,000 kilometres (2,500 miles) from north to south, the terrain of Chile is extremely diverse, and ranges from the Atacama Desert, one of driest on this planet ... (Photo by Oscar Ruf Wilson)

... to mountains towering 6,000 metres (22,000ft) high, covered with snow all year. (Photo by Oscar Ruf Wilson)

this place was covered by glaciers which strongly eroded the reliefs. The intermediate depression disappears beneath the sea, but the Cordillera of the Coast gives rise to a series of archipelagos like Chiloé and the Chonos, before disappearing at the level of the peninsula of Taitao, towards the 47th parallel. To the east of the Cordillera there are additional plains around the Straits of Magellan off the Tierra del Fuego.

Chiloé and its neighbouring islands are among the most underdeveloped regions of the country: agriculture and shellfish collection are the main activities. On the contrary, the Magallanes is the most developed part of Chilean Patagonia and Tierra del Fuego. Sheep-raising ranches which have exported wool since the late 19th century, and oil and natural gas, which have been exploited since 1945, are the pillars of its economy. These activities, combined with meat-packing plants and the trading functions of Punta Arenas, have made this one of the more modern parts of Chile.

Due to its remoteness, Chile was never an attractive place for migrants and there was never a massive immigration of Spaniards and

Araucaria, a genus of evergreen coniferous trees, is one of typical plants in Chile. (Photo by Oscar Ruf Wilson)

the Portuguese, like in other parts of Latin America. Relatively sizeable groups of Italians, Irish, French, Greeks, Germans, English, Scots, Croats, Palestinians, and Poles moved in after the independence. As of 1970, the population was thus a multiethnic society of only about 9,780,000, of whom some 40% had Native American ancestry, about 5% were descendants of Asian immigrants, while over 50% were people with European immigrant backgrounds. The official language is Spanish, but German and English are still spoken to great extent in various parts of the country, as are several indigenous languages. Over 70% of the population identify themselves as Roman Catholic, and about 15% as evangelical or as followers of other non-Catholic Christian churches.

Chile has important mining resources including copper, iron, nitrates and other concentrated minerals, and these contribute to the national exports and domestic industrial development. Mining initially developed with the help of US investments in the early 20th Century, and meanwhile transformed Chile into the World's largest producer and exporter of copper. The country is dotted with major mines, including several in the north (Chuquicamata and El Salvador), and others in the Andes of northern central regions (El Teniente and Andina). Major iron mines are El Tofo and El Romeral, in northern central Chile, while manganese, silver, gold, and molybdenum (a metal derived from the large copper deposits) are exploited too. Among non-metallic minerals, sulphur, gypsum, lithium, and limestone are moderately exploited. Nitrate deposits occur in the northern interior desert.

Chile in the 20th Century

During the first two decades of the 20th Century, the economic development provoked discontent in the population. The strong migration of the rural population to the cities left the migrants in poor living conditions, causing overpopulation and health problems. A politically active working class developed in the saltpetre mines, but also in public enterprises and factories. Working conditions were generally poor and the 'social question' expressed itself in the form of strikes and demonstrations – frequently suppressed in blood by the military – but also the foundation of labour unions and the birth of the Worker's Socialist Party (Partido Obrero Socialista, POS) in 1912, which was transformed into the Communist Party in 1922. On the other hand, expansion of the railroad network and booming commerce favoured the formation of an urban middle-class. This was attracted to the Radical Party established in 1888. The emergence of these new political forces illustrated the inability of the ruling class to solve problems of the emerging industrial society: this proved unable to reform the country, and only continued provoking continuous political instability.[7]

The Liberals won the elections of 1920, resulting in the appointment of Arturo Alessandri Palma, former Minister of Interior, as President. Palma tried to push through his reforms, but the Senate blocked his initiatives causing much anger among mid-ranking military officers[8]. In 1924, these intervened to force a parliamentary vote on social reforms. Alessandri resigned, but the military returned him to power in 1925. Alessandri reacted by developing a new constitution, which established a presidential republic, separated church from the state, codified the new labour and welfare legislation, and remained valid until 1973.

The constitution of 1925 did not end the permanent political crisis. In 1927, General Ibáñez was elected the president in place of Alessandri. Although receiving plenty of support within the population, he rapidly turned authoritarian – even more so when

Port of Valparaíso, as seen on a postcard from 19th Century. (Carlos Brandt)

Chilean soldiers guarded all of the elections in the 1940s and 1950s, making sure these would be run smoothly. (Albert Grandolini Collection)

The military out on the streets during the nation-wide strike of 1956. (Albert Grandolini Collection)

facing the global economic crisis of 1929, which hit Chile very hard.[9] Facing massive demonstrations, Ibáñez resigned in 1931, and traditional political groups – presided over by Juan Estaban Montero Rodríguez – regained power. The respite was rather short: when every attempt to solve the economic crisis failed, the Coquimbo Naval Squadron launched an uprising on 4 June 1932, while a committee including Marmaduque Grove, Carlos Dávila and Eugenio Matte proclaimed the Socialist Republic of Chile. The latter lasted for exactly 12 days: following additional turmoil, Dávilla took over as president for something like three months – before Alessandri was re-installed as president.

In the wake of one coup attempt and further changes of the government, Alessandri was re-elected in 1932 with the support of the centrist and right-wing parties. Although he ruled with the help of a pluralist cabinet, the Radicals began leaning towards the left-

A row of M3 Stuart tanks of the Chilean military on the streets of Santiago during the general strike of January 1956. (Albert Grandolini Collection)

wing political spectrum during this period, and the division between them and the right-wing movement resulted in political violence. This culminated in the Ranquil massacre, and then the State of Siege, proclaimed by Alessandri in February 1936.[10]

Despite many calamities, the Chilean president eventually managed to restore the economy and remained in power until the end of his legal mandate in 1938.

Meanwhile, a new political coalition emerged, in 1936, including the Popular Front (comprising Radicals, Socialists, and Communists). This won the elections of 1938 and formed a new government presided by Pedro Aguirre Cerda.[11] Inspired by the 'New Deal' of the US President Franklin D. Roosevelt, his program emphasised education and industrialisation, reduction of imports and decrease of the trade deficit, and increased production of consumer goods. The state intervened not only in the economy, but also within the sectors of public health and education. Slowly growing wealth accelerated the rural exodus and the population of the capital soon grew to over 1 million.

Chile declared neutrality during both World Wars, and retained good relations with Italy. Indeed, while most of the population supported the Allies, significant segments expressed their sympathies for the Nazi Germany. Relations with the Axis-powers were broken only in 1943, and Chile declared war on Japan two years later, becoming the last nation to join World War II. This conflict, and the following Korean War, benefited Chilean the economy greatly, as they dramatically increased the demand for copper, in turn prompting an expansion of public education and industrial development.

Meanwhile, the political stability began to crumble. In 1946, Gabriel González Videla was elected president of a government that included members of the Communist Party of Chile (PCCh). However, the communist success and increased agitation by trade unions caused a political crisis that was only resolved when all the PCCh-members resigned from the government, which in turn broke its diplomatic relations with the Soviet Union. The miners' unions reacted by a major strike and violent demonstrations, which in turn prompted the government to declared a state of siege and outlaw the PCCh. This brought no respite, then not only a failed military revolt led by former president Ibáñez, but also major social upheaval followed. By 1951, almost all sectors of the economy were hit by strikes. Manifesting their opposition to traditional power-brokers in the country, the population elected Ibáñez – supported by the Agrarian-Labour Party – in 1952.

Once in power, Ibáñez proved a populist. He supported the creation of the Unified Workers Central (*Central Unica de Trabajadores*, CUT) and lifted the ban on the PCCh. However, his mandate was marked by the next economic crisis, as result of which he lost support in the population. In an attempt to recover the situation, Ibáñez adopted

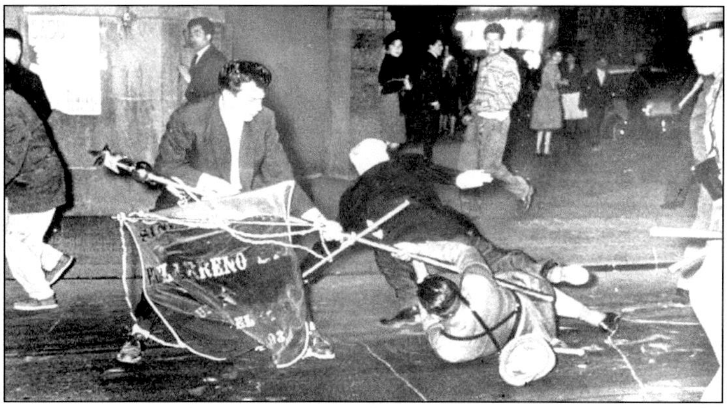

A scene from the riots in Santiago de Chile in 1960. (Albert Grandolini Collection)

liberalization of the economy, but this only triggered additional strikes and mass protests, during which up to 20 people were killed, in 1957.[12]

A year later, Jorge Alessandri Rodríguez – a former senator and son of Arturo Alessandri – was elected president.[13] He governed with the help of a coalition of liberals and conservatives, with a program favouring free enterprise and foreign investment. By the end of his mandate, the right-wing parties were weakened to the point where their electoral power was cut in half. In response, the conservatives created the Nationalist Party (Partido Nacional, PN) in 1965.

Meanwhile, the Christian Democratic Party (PDC), a centrist movement leaning towards the left wing, founded in 1957, gained in popularity, while the PCCh regained some of its former fame. The two blocks soon realized they had several common objectives – including the one of weakening the old economic and political oligarchy, and launching a reform in the chronically underdeveloped agrarian sector.

The elections of 1964 thus took place in an atmosphere of 'cold war', and with leftists dominating the political scene. Salvador Allende Gossens led a coalition of several parties, with PDC's Eduardo Montalva Frei appearing as his only serious opponent. Frightened by Allende, not only the Chilean right-wing parties, but even the USA began supporting Frei, who propagated deep reforms – and eventually won 56% of the vote with the slogan, 'Revolution in Freedom'.[14]

Frei launched numerous reforms. In July 1966, he partially nationalised the copper mines by acquiring 51% of shares from major US companies. In addition, he furthered the development of local industry and, in 1967, introduced an agricultural reform that expropriated all farms with more than 80 hectare. Peasant cooperatives were established on the newly won land, and the state taught these cooperatives advanced farming techniques. However, this reform progressed slowly because of its costly emphasis on better housing, improved equipment, and irrigation. Thus, though effective and successful, Frei's initiatives provoked discontent and bolstered violent political opposition. By 1967, his government was facing ever more fierce opposition from the Left and the Right, with one side considering his actions too timid, and the other despotic, respectively. Rumours about a possible coup began making circles and indeed: on 29 October 1969, General Roberto Viaux ordered the Tacna Artillery Regiment to march on Santiago. This coup attempt, called *Tacnazo*, proved a failure, but it did reflect the gravity of the situation prior to the elections of 1970.

CHAPTER 2

CHILE BETWEEN HOPE AND FEARS, 1970-1973

Coming from a middle-class family, Salvador Allende Gossens was born on 26 June 1908 in Santiago. He spent his first ten years in Tacna, a port of Chile. At 11, he left for Santiago to study at the National Institute, a prestigious secondary school where he spent one year before rejoining his family, now in the southern city of Valdivia. In 1922, a new job posting brought the family to Valparaíso, the city that Allende would later claim as his own, and where he finished his secondary studies at the Liceo Eduardo de la Barra.

Young Allende was attracted by the political ideas of Juan Demarchi, an Italian anarchist and immigrant whose shop was in front of the Allende house.[15] The young man began reading revolutionary literature. Above all, he finished his secondary studies in 1924, as the country entered a prolonged period of tumultuous change.

Allende postponed his university studies to join the military. While military service was compulsory, the middle-class easily avoided it. Allende served in the cavalry, first at Viña del Mar and then in Tacna.[16] Realising the military did not suit him, he returned to civilian life to study medicine, beginning a six-year course at the University of Chile in March 1926.[17] These were times of tumult on the local political scene, which included a strong student movement. Allende was thus never far from the events. While living in Recoleta, a 'very humble district' of Santiago, he worked during the day, and read Karl Marx's 'Das Kapital', and various works by Lenin and Trotsky by night.[18] Furthermore, his medical training informed him of the necessity of improving the health of the poor, and developed his dedication for socialism.

University student politics were often training grounds for later political careers, like Fidel Castro in Cuba, and Allende entered this arena in 1927 as president of the notably activist Association of Medical Students. Three years later, he helped revive the Student Federation of the University of Chile (FECH), shut down by Ibañéz in 1926. Allende's participation in 'Avance' – a student group largely composed of socialists and communists that attempted to push the FECH to the left – proved formative. In mid-1931, as the world depression caused the bankruptcy of Chile, Ibañéz resigned in the face of unrelenting economic problems and mounting street protests. The students in 'Avance' actively participated, calling for the creation of 'Soviets' of workers, peasants, soldiers and students. The organization asked its members approve this position, and virtually all of them did – except Allende, who was expelled.[19]

Allende graduated in 1933, after a short period of imprisonment for his activism. He returned to Valparaíso and became an assistant pathologist. He was, meanwhile, a dedicated Marxist but never dogmatic: when, the Socialist Republic was found by Grove, Hurtado, and Dávila in June 1932, he refused to support it, insisting that electoral politics and constitutional democracy were the best ways of establishing socialism, and fostering economic and social development.

In 1933, Allende was involved in the creation of the Socialist Party (PS) in Valparaíso.[20] This was formed by a mixture of expelled

A pro-Allende demo staged during the campaign of 1964. (Biblioteca del Congreso Nacional)

Allende during a public speech given in the course of the campaign of 1964. (Biblioteca del Congreso Nacional)

communists, social-democrats, but also Trotskyists, anarcho-syndicalists and independents. The PS never imposed doctrinal orthodoxy like the 'dictatorship of the proletariat': it was committed to state-ownerships as the means of production, to anti-imperialism, and to advancing the rights of workers and peasants.

Three years later, Allende initiated the establishment of the Popular Front – a coalition of radicals, socialists, and communists – and in 1937 was elected deputy in the Chambers of Deputies. In 1939, still only 31 years old, Allende lead the campaign of the candidate of the Popular Front in the presidential elections, and then entered the government of Cerda as Minister of Health. During his mandate, he distributed free medicine against venereal diseases, and allocated a budget of two million pesos for public health centres and dental service in schools.[21]

By 1943-1944, Allende was general secretary of the PS, before being elected senator in 1945. He became the symbol of moderate socialism, advocated social welfare programs, propagated rights of workers and peasants, and the nationalisation of US-owned copper companies. As a Chairman of the Senate's Health Committee, he wrote legislation that consolidated many of Chile's health care programs within the National Health Service. At the same time, he developed strong ideological differences with leaders of the PCCh, but also blasted Pesident González Videla for banning the Communists in 1948.[22]

Allende presented himself for the first time to the presidency of Chile in 1952 as representative of the People's Front (*Frente del Pueblo*), which obtained only 5% of the votes. Nevertheless, his campaign attracted nation-wide attention and helped him strengthen relations between the Socialists and the Communists. In 1958, he was candidate for the FRAP and won nearly 29% of the vote while arguing for an expansion of his party to include the Radicals and the PDC. Allende ran for presidential elections in 1964 again, this time under the colours of the FRAP. By this time, the Cuban Revolution caused major shifts in the political landscape of the whole of Latin America, and thus, in 1959, he visited Cuba to meet Fidel Castro.[23] Henceforth, the Chilean right-wingers accused him of preparing a similar Marxist, or even Maoist, dictatorship in Chile.

Regardless how much support for Cuba – and the armed insurgencies from Bolivia to Vietnam – Allende expressed, he never abandoned his decision to bring Chile to socialism along a constitutional path. Unsurprisingly, he continued to disagree with the far-left wings of various parties (especially the Movement of the Revolutionary Left, MIR), but also that of the PS. Such disagreements were another reason for Allende's defeat during elections of 1964.[24]

Election Campaign of 1970

Although the atmosphere in Chile of 1970 was extremely politicised, and the standpoints of different political parties opposed each other strongly, the election campaign came forward without violence. Allende established himself as the key propagator of the 'Chilean Way to Socialism' – which was based on peaceful transition through wining elections and then pursuing the policy of nationalisation of copper-related industry, and the creation of 'popular power' through an agricultural reform. In itself achieving this position proved anything other than easy because the Popular Unity (UP) coalition meanwhile consisted of very different parties – including the PS, the PCCh, the Radicals, the Social-Democrats, the MAPU (the leftist breakaway from the Christian Democrats) and the API. Many youngsters saw Allende as a 'man of the past', and found it hard to forget his three earlier defeats. Even in Allende's own party, many had abandoned all hope in the politics he propagated. Indeed, members of the Central Committee of the PS – which was declared 'Marxist' in 1967 – opposed Allende's selection as presidential candidate. What saved him was the nomination by the rank and file of regional parties, and the support of the PCCh.[25]

Unsurprisingly, considering the potential importance of the coming elections, all candidates began receiving support from abroad. According to the CIA, Allende should have received up to US$ 350,000 from Cuba. According to the Soviet defector Mithrokin, Moscow sponsored Allende with a further $400,000 – although it turned out that all of this money was actually donated to the PCCh. Furthermore, various parties of the UP coalition might have received up to $15,000 from the former East Germany, while the CIA spent between $800,000 and $1 million to support other candidates. Foremost between the latter were members of the Right, meanwhile consolidated into the PN, led by Jorge Alessandri (who received about $350,000), and the Christian Democrats, led by Radomiro Tomic.[26] Tomic propagated Christian humanism and pledged to deepen the social reforms like the 'Chileanisation of copper resources'.[27] Alessandri was promising his supporters the return to the liberal economic system, the restoration of order, and a regression of reforms in agricultural sector.

The UP and the PDC staged mass rallies in support of their candidates, bringing together thousands of people, but Alessandri's staff – much of which was confident of his victory – preferred no such acts out of the concern that its 74-years-old and sluggish candidate might not perform favourably. The only big action staged on behalf of Alessandri was boycotted by national television and thus widely considered a 'failure'. The PN and the Christian-Democrats were greatly irritated when the Commander-in-Chief (C-in-C) of the Chilean Armed Forces, Major-General René Schneider, stated in

Supporters of the UP Coalition as seen during the campaign of 1970. (Albert Grandolini Collection)

Allende during his inauguration – together with top commanders of all three branches of the Chilean military. (Biblioteca del Congreso Nacional)

an interview that, in the case that neither of candidates obtained an absolute majority, the military would follow advice of the Congress and the postulates of the fundamental charter. Namely, tradition in the Chilean politics was for the party with relative majority to pick the president.

Eventually, elections were held on 4 September 1970, in a climate of peace and order. Results were published shortly after midnight: Allende won 36.6% of the vote, Alessandri 35.3%, and Tomic 28.1%.

The National Congress was left without a choice but to ratify Allende's triumph in the polls: while he did not obtain the absolute majority, members of the parliament had the right to chose between the first two relative majorities. Following corresponding agreements with the PDC, Salvador Allende was elected the President of the Republic on 4 November 1970.[28]

Allende's 'Chilean way to Socialism' thus not only obtained a clear majority on the polls but was to open the way urgently necessary reforms.

US Interventions: Projects Track I and Track II

This first-ever electoral victory of a candidate with a clearly socialist program in a non-communist country severely disturbed the perceived 'balance of the Cold War'. Indeed, in Washington it gave rise to panic. The administration of the US President Richard Nixon expected an easy victory for Alessandri and thus never provided as much help to Alessandri as it did to Frei in 1964.[29]

Unwilling 'to accept another Cuba', and always critical of late president John Kennedy's failure to prevent the consolidation of Fidel Castro's rule, Nixon ordered a meeting of his top security advisers in the Oval Office, on 15 September 1970. Yelling, 'That son of a bitch!' at the triumph of the Chilean Marxist, the US president was convinced that Allende was a new Castro, that Chile would soon be subjected to a Marxist dictatorship, and thus become a model for what might happen in France and Italy. With this prospect being a nightmare for the US government, he decided to prevent Allende's ratification by the Congress of Chile.[30]

Thus came into being the plan for the operation code-named 'Project Track I'. This aimed to 'politically persuade' – i.e. bribe – members of the Chile's Congress to vote against Allende and for Alessandri instead. In the next step of this operation, the Congress would then force Alessandri's resignation, thus provoking new presidential elections, during which Eduardo Frei was to be the sole candidate of the PDC and the Right. Furthermore, and to make sure, the CIA also evaluated the opportunities for an intervention by the Chilean military in order to prevent Allende's inauguration as president.[31]

Related activity inside Chile is known to have been initiated already: on 6 September 1970, Alessandri's assistant called the PDC to support his ratification by the Congress, and thus 'save Chile from Marxism'.[32] However, this plot proved a failure right from the start: the PDC and the UP found agreement based on a secret pact between Allende and Tomic, on condition of Allende signing the 'Statute of Constitutional Guarantees'. The Project Track I thus fell apart before it was even launched.

Despite this failure, Nixon continued his efforts to prevent Allende's ratification. He requested Richard Helms, director of the CIA, to 'save Chile' with the 'best men we have', in complete disregard of 'risks involved'. Correspondingly, a 'Special Task Force' was set up, lead by Henry Kissinger (Nixon's National Security Adviser), to develop and implement the Project Track II, the goal of which was to create a climate of instability in Chile and push the army into a coup.[33]

The Project Track II faced a significant obstacle in form of Major-General Schneider, who had guaranteed the loyalty of the military and its support for the constitutional process. Indeed, Henry Hecksher, the CIA's station chief in Santiago, cabled to Washington:

'General Schneider is the main barrier to all plans for the military to take over."

The reply from the USA was without ambiguity, and explained that it was, 'more important than ever to remove him'[34]

The Project Track II thus first focused on eliminating Schneider.

With the CIA refusing to launch an outright intervention, the Americans depended on several leading figures from the Right – foremost those terrified of Allende's victory. Primary amongst these was Agustín Edwards Eastman, owner of the newspaper *El Mercurio*, who fled to the USA and asked for Nixon's support in destabilisation of the new government. It is known that Edwards met Kissinger and John Mitchell, the US Attorney General, for breakfast on 15 September 1970. Next, he met Richard Helms to, amongst others items, discuss 'the possibility of a military action'.[35] Understanding they could not rely upon active military officers – who remained loyal to the so-called 'Schneider doctrine'.[36] Therefore, they turned to retired officers and right-wing activists. Amongst others, Edwards was already in contact with Major-General Robert Viaux, leader of the Tacnazo from 1969, and with several extremists from the PN.

Project Track II thus included a plot for Schneider's kidnapping and his sequestration in the hope this might trigger a military action that would end the constitutional process. On 20 October 1970, the US military attaché in Santiago handed over the necessary bribe and three firearms to Chilean conspirators. However, when this attack was

Richard Milhous Nixon, President of the USA, proved one of most fierce – and most powerful – opponents of Allende's government outside the country. (Wikimedia Commons)

launched two days later, Schneider defended himself and pulled out his gun. In return, he was shot and mortally wounded. While causing a great shock in Chile – notably within the military – this did not prevent Allende's ratification by the Congress.[37]

Even then, Nixon – 'brandmarked' by the Cuban revolution that cost him the presidential elections of 1960 – never stopped plotting against Allende. On 6 November 1970, he ordered his administration to give Chile an economic 'cold turkey'. Along with this directive, a covert action plan was developed along which the US intelligence agency was to start financing anti-Allende media, launch clandestine operations against the UP, and spread fake news abroad about Cuban and Soviet involvement in Chile.[38]

Chilean Way to Socialism.

Unaware of the US plots, Allende spent the days following his election with explaining his projects. He insisted he would 'respect the rights of all Chileans', but left no doubts about his intentions:

'When I enter La Moneda, I will carry out the historic commitment to make the Popular Unity's program a reality.'[39]

Facing an economic recession marked by high inflation and 8.4% unemployment, he entrusted the management of the economy to Pedro Vuskovic, ordering him to implement the transition from capitalism to socialism in late 1970. Only weeks later, he explained the aims of his program to Regis Debray: a centralized economy, far-reaching land reform, collectivisation of a major portion of national production, dialogue with the workers, and establishment of new social relations.[40]

Some of Allende's and Vuskovic's first decisions were related to the policy of expansionary aggregate demand: at the cost of significantly increased government's expenditures, they first increased wages, hoping to prompt higher rates of money creation and circulation.

Members of the PCCh during a demonstration in support of Allende. Despite certain ideological differences, most Chilean communists were staunch supporters of the Marxist president. (Albert Grandolini Collection)

Furthermore, they began nationalising companies considered vital to the economy and expropriated a number of enterprises through the procedure called 'government intervention', and then nationalized a number of foreign companies that were considered as in possession of diverse monopolies.

With such measures including little new – the process of nationalising the copper industry was initiated already by Frei's UP government – they received the unanimous support of most politicians, and on 15 July 1971 the related law was approved by the Congress.

By the end of 1971, the state controlled more than 80% of the total mining production. It had acquired about 70% of its targeted industrial companies, and a similar percentage of the banking sector. The situation reached the point where workers in companies that remained in private hands began calling for the nationalisation of these, too, in the hope of getting better pay.[41]

Allende's Early Success

Tight price controls and the sudden rise of wages were likely to cause inflation. However, because up to 20% of Chilean production capacity was underutilised, manufacturers quickly increased their production. In turn, this generated an economic growth and a rapid decrease of unemployment. Allende's 'experiment' thus appeared to work: the first year of his administration was marked by low inflation and an economic growth of 8%. This development not only raised the popularity of his government, but attracted lots of attention abroad too: not only that the UP won 49.73% of vote during municipal elections in 1971, but the communist poet Pablo Neruda won the Nobel Prize for Literature.[42]

In the agricultural sector, Allende's government continued and then extended Frei's reforms. By the end of 1971, up to two million hectares were expropriated; a further nine followed by mid-1972. However, 'land occupation' caused tensions and then violence between peasants and landowners. The first to be killed was Rolando Matus, a small landowner in the south of the country, who opposed the occupation of his land by force. He became a martyr for the Right, who denounced the government's support as 'illegal actions', and prompted this party

The reorganisation of the Chilean economy initiated by Allende was successful early on. However, by 1971 it caused a major economic crisis – and major shortages of basic consumer goods. So-called 'bread lines' became a usual scene in all of Chile by 1973. (Albert Grandolini Collection)

to name its militant wing after him.

First Problems

Although foreign mining companies were compensated (even though with the subtraction of the 'excessive profits' realized since 1955), the act of nationalisation was another pretext for Washington to reinforce its economic war against Chile. Indeed, before long the Nixon administration was issuing public calls for a boycott of Allende, and imposed an embargo on imports of Chilean copper.

Further problems were created by Allende's and Vuskovic's decisions. The continuously increasing fiscal deficit continued to grow at an accelerated pace – from 3.5% of the GDP in 1970 to 9.8% in 1971, to 13% in 1972 and 24% in 1973.[43] Financial policy was obviously out of control as the public sector credit grew by 124%, while foreign currency reserves dropped from US$394 million in 1970 to US$163 million in 1971, forcing the government to suspend servicing its external debt. Nevertheless, during the first quarter of 1973, foreign currency reserves reached less than two months' worth of imports.[44] The increase of wages, and price controls further provoked a contraction of corporate profits and the first signs of shortages appeared in the second quarter of 1971.

The economic crisis continued to spread during 1972, by which time the public deficit was increasing and the inflation galloping at 225%. Worse was to follow in 1973, when the inflation reached 606%. High inflation decreased real wages by 11% in 1972 and 38% in 1973, in turn resulting in less consumer spending. The deficit reached 25% of GNP and the external debt increased by US$253 million. Eventually, the production levels dropped, consumer products began disappearing from the stores, and the black market boomed. To struggle against these shortages, the UP instituted the JAP (Juntas de Abastecimiento y Precios or Committees of Supplies and Prices) who requisitioned goods and forcibly opened private shops; a new factor of contention with the right who accused them of damaging the private market.[45]

The Polarization of Society

On 1 December 1971, female oppositional activists organized the 'March of the Pots and Pans' to downtown Santiago – to protest shortages of food and basic products, and to signal the existence of the well-organized, mass-based movement that the UP's foes lacked at earlier times.[46] This march signalled a reconstruction of the Chilean political landscape.

The PN was, meanwhile, the primary opposition party and at odds with the UP ever since its parliamentaries refused to ratify Allende's presidency. However, at no moment over the next three years had the right-wing party proved to have the weight necessary to stop the 'Chilean Way into Socialism'. The only means to construct a solid opposition to Allende was finding an agreement with the PDC – which became possible when Tomic distanced from the president, following the murder of Edmundo Pérez Zujovic (former minister in Frei's government) by the ultra-leftist party named the Organized Vanguard of the People (VOP), in June 1971.[47]

Understanding that the government was unable to control the ultra-leftists, the PDC and the PN joined their efforts during the complementary elections for the deputy governor of Valparaíso. Although the PDC candidate won thanks to PN's support, this alliance failed to consolidate immediately due to various differences. Only after three failed attempts were the oppositional parties able to cooperate and start raising accusations against various members of the government. Their cooperation was finally consolidated only during the complementary elections for the deputy governor of Linares and the senators in the provinces of O'Higgins and Colchagua in January 1972.

Castro's Scepticism

Late in 1971, Fidel Castro visited Chile for three weeks. Travelling all over the country, he upset the opponents of the UP, especially because his travels coincided with the first shortages – including those of sugar. Privately, the Cuban leader expressed his scepticism for Allende's peaceful politics. On 2 December 1971, the CIA reported to Washington that Castro said,

> There is very little possibility of building a Marxist state in Chile if violence is not used.[48]

Castro's scepticism was shared by many of Chilean leftists, especially the MIR and the PS's left wing. The PS supported government strategy during the first year of Allende's mandate although its leader, Carlos Altamirano, followed Lenin's teaching to the letter and went on the record to state, 'Only by destroying the military bureaucratic apparatus of the bourgeois state can [we] consolidate the socialist revolution.'[49] While acting as an intermediary between the 'insurrectional tendency' of left-wing activists and the government early on, Altamirano's role grew increasingly difficult over the time. The MIR acceded to Allende's demands to refrain from armed actions, but mirisistas – the MIR's membership- intensified their actions, such as the occupation of arable land and factories. Aware of the fact that the government refused to use force against them, other far-left factions attempted to establish themselves in control of forces unleashed by Allende's election too. For example, workers in industries not slated for the public sector forced Allende's hand by occupying their factories and demanding expropriation[50].

Gradually, new, ever more extreme movements came into being. In 1972, the Industrial Belt (Cordón Industrial) Cerillos-Maipú came into being, where workers from neighbouring companies began coordinating the tasks of different factories. This example spread across the country and prompted farmers to start organizing 'communal commands' that integrated such social sectors in the vicinity as trade unions, farmers, settlers, students and the JAPs.[51] Before long, dozens of such groups established themselves in effective control over specific installations, parts of cities, towns, villages or entire territories, in which workers and farmers had all the power: they knew the area and the terrain, they knew what levels of access they had to control, and they combined their resources at their own discretion.

Groups of the industrial belt and communal commands played

Fidel Castro with Salvador Allende during the three-week long visit to Chile in late 1971. (Albert Grandolini Collection)

Castro with the C-in-C of the Chilean Military, Major-General Carlos Prats. (Albert Grandolini Collection)

a very important role in the nationalisation of different companies and the land occupation. For example, while the government planned to extend the public sector to about 91 companies in 1972, they incorporated about 250 enterprises.[52] The workers acted with audacity and rudeness unseen since the days of the Socialist Republic of Grove. They appointed and replaced their leaders on short notice, requisitioned trucks, buses and other means of transport to maintain production and distribution, and they controlled supermarkets. They controlled the streets too, and introduced actions of 'popular justice' to sanction, for example, the expulsion of those known to have beaten women.[53]

By August 1973, the number of industrial belts grew to 110, while there were dozens of communal commands around the country. In Santiago, they had the capacity to mobilize more than 100,000 supporters. Unsurprisingly, for many Chileans they represented the biggest danger for democracy, the rule of law and private property. Because of ill-defined relations between them and the government, they represented a significant threat for the stability of the entire country – even more so once the far-left began calling for the creation of a popular army, in turn causing fears within the Chilean military.[54]

The Strike of October 1972

A worsening economic situation and rumours of nationalization of transport companies caused a strike of truckers in the province of Aysé, starting on 1 October 1972. Eight days later, the National Confederation of Truck Owners (Confederación Nacional de Dueños de Camiones CNDC), led by Leon Vilarín, with the support of other guilds, called for an indefinite national strike, aggravating the problems of distribution of goods. The strike was supported by the CIA, which continued conspiring to bring down the UP government.[55]

In response, the government decided to take legal action against the organizers of the strike, which was described by Interior Minister Jaime Suarez as 'political, illegal and seditious'. León Vilarín and other transport leaders were arrested and transferred to the Public Jail of Santiago on the night of 10 October. The truckers responded to these measures by blocking the country's main roads on 12 October, causing the shortage of fuel and other essential goods. Allende reacted by declaring a state of emergency in 18 provinces.[56]

However, his reaction failed to reverse the situation. On the contrary, it provoked discontent and additional protests. Gradually, the opposition and other professional guilds pleaded for mobilization; the small shopkeepers confederation (Confedech), led by Rafael Cumsille; the Confederation of Small Industry and Craft (Conupia); the Confederation of Production and Trade (CPC), and the Association of Owners of Microbuses and Taxibuses of Private Collective Locomotion all went to the streets. On 17 October, they were joined by the Medical College, the associations of engineers, lawyers, dentists, teachers, port workers, pilots of the National Air Line of Chile (Línea Aérea Nacional de Chile, LAN), and the Federation of Students of the Catholic University of Chile (FEUC) joined the strike. The country was virtually paralysed.[57]

Two days later, León Vilarín announced the preparation of a list of petitions to the government that, in Sergio Bitar's words, "[revealed] that, after a trade union image, there was a vast political operation".[58] The next day the *Nacional Commando de Defensa Gremial* was formed, which brought together a large part of the employer's confederations. The *Nacional Commando* published its demands in a document known as *El pliego de Chile*, originally published in the newspaper *El Mercurio* on 22 October, and replicated by the rest of the opposition media.

A demonstration of the Socialist Youth in downtown Santiago in 1973. (Albert Grandolini Collection)

Carabinerios reacting to one of the student demonstrations against Allende in August 1973. (Albert Grandolini Collection)

Armed peasants guarding an occupied estate in Cautin province. (Mark Lepko Collection)

Following negotiations with the government, the strike ended on 24 October, named the 'Day of Silence'.[59] In response to the requests of protesters, Allende appointed several military officers as new ministers, including Major-General Carlos Prats as Minister of Interior, Rear Admiral Ismael Huerta as Minister of Public Works, and Brigadier General Claudio Sepúlveda as Minister of Mining. This cabinet lasted until parliamentary elections of March 1973.

In the course of the latter campaign, the opposition grouped into the Confederation of Democracy (*Confederación de la Democracia*, CODE) and aimed to obtain two-thirds of seats in the Congress – which would enable it to bring a constitutional charge against Allende and dismissal of the president. However, the UP won 43.5% of the vote

Demonstration of workers at the Caletones Mining Centre, near Rancagua, in 1973. (Albert Grandolini Collection)

and CODE 54.6%. The UP parties, presented in a single list, were able to increase their representation with three deputies and one senator.[60] In this way, Allende was safe from impeachment and the opposition lost the last means of overturning the government by lawful means. It seemed that only force could solve the crisis and unblock the situation.

The Spread of Violence, Economic and Political Chaos

During 1973, the old capitalist structures of Chile were crumbling without being replaced by new relations of production or centralized planning. By September, the economy was dislocated and in a runaway recession. There were 507 companies in the hands of the state or taken by its workers, including large industry, banking and services. Thousands of farms were in different phases of occupation by the peasants. The inflation rose to 508.1%. The lack of supply and the black market competed with a distribution apparatus that was broken by opponents, without the JAP managing to replace it. Daily life was a round of queuing for goods in short supply. The trade deficit was growing and the lack of foreign exchange curtailed the acquisition of consumer and capital goods. Fiscal accounts were dropping due to falling revenues.[61]

On the political scene, the situation was in a stalemate. On 11 June, Congress passed the Hamilton-Fuentealba constitutional reform by 106 votes, which safeguarded farms with less than 40 hectares and provided guarantees to private companies. Allende refused to promulgate the entire reform arguing that the law would self-expropriate any hectare that exceeded the established minimum and only published the part of this law in which the PDC didn't have great differences with the UP. This decision was based on the power of the president to veto any law requiring two thirds of votes in the Congress. The opposition considered this act unconstitutional and the Supreme Court (Contraloría General de la República) supported its point of view, creating a conflict between the powers of the executive and the legislative.

Allende had two options to solve this crisis: a nation-wide referendum, or an alliance with the PDC. With Cardinal Raul Silva Henríquez acting as intermediary, he entered negotiations with the president of the PDC Patricio Aylwin – but without success. According to Henríquez, the reason was the intransigence of the UP, Frei's refusal of dialogue, and Aylwin's demands for ministers with military backgrounds to receive broader powers than those from UP parties.[62]

The result was an even deeper rift within Chilean society and a significant rise in violence on the streets. A government project, called Unified National Scholl, would reform the educational system – from one based on values of capitalism, to one based on values of the 'new

Allende, among his supporters, sits below a photograph of Che Guevara. (Albert Grandolini Collection)

A demonstration of Young Fascists in Santiago in 1973. (Albert Grandolini Collection)

man', and 'life-long education'. This prompted a violent reaction from right-wing student groups. The Federation of Students of the Catholic University (FEUC) called for the defence of educational freedom against what it called the, 'instrument of political awareness of Marxism'. Outright fist-fights with communist and socialist students erupted, and the chaos was furthered by the general lack of supplies, land grabs, and armed gangs. As the violence unleashed by radical groups – including supporters and opponents of the government – continued to spread, the climate of confrontation reached all spheres of the society, including the elites, which had always kept themselves outside the social, economic, and political convulsions in the country. Clashes between different political groups resulted in dozens killed and hundreds of injured, but became more frequent as the CIA instigated a campaign of bomb attacks in a further attempt to destabilise Allende's government. Several high-voltage tension lines, oil pipelines, and embassies (including those of Cuba and the USSR), as well as radio stations and headquarters of left-wing political parties, were bombed, and left-wing militants assassinated.[63]

Economic collapse and political intransigence interacted and reinforced each other. The famous Chilean constitutional system proved too weak to contain political conflict in which neither the government, nor the opposition were prepared to make major concessions in order to safeguard the system. The opposition indulged in a whole series of measures designed to obstruct the executive: measures which, if not illegal, certainly violated the conventions of the congressional system. The government too employed measures of dubious legality. Such actions re-enforced mutual suspicions and made it difficult to see any way out of the impasse. With both government and opposition lined up against each other in bitter confrontation, with the economy out of control, with increasing violence, there was little prospect of a peaceful solution.

An anti-Fascist demonstration of the Socialist Youth, in 1973. (Albert Grandolini Collection)

Participants of the last pro-UP-coalition demonstration in Santiago, staged on 4 September 1973. (Albert Grandolini Collection)

During the summer of 1973, Allende proposed a nation-wide referendum about a new constitution as the way out. However, the Congress blocked this attempt, prompting the president to talk about ways to bypassing it. Eventually, Allende had decided to announce the plebiscite on Tuesday, 11 September 1973, during a speech at the State Technical University (Universidad Técnica del Estado, UTE) in Santiago. Instead, it was the weapons that were to speak on that day.

CHAPTER 3

ALLENDE, THE ARMED FORCES, AND THE LEFT-WING'S MILITARY POLITICS

During the times of the Spanish colonial rule, the Chilean territory was the scene of a struggle between the conquistadors and the native population, the Araucanians. For the Spanish Crown, the area represented a strategic position at the entry point to the Pacific Ocean. In defence of its possessions, an army under the command of Alfonso de Ribera was established in Concepción, on 22 January 1604, by order of Philipp III.[64] During later stages of the colonial period, and in the 19th Century in particular, Chile depended principally on a militia of about 16,000 for its defence.[65]

Early during the country's war of independence, following the mutiny of Figueroa and the seizure of power by José Miguel Carrera, the first 'National Army' was established, on 5 December 1810, by order of the first national government. Based on the militia called the 'Army of the Captaincy General of Chile', this consisted of one battalion of infantry, two squadrons of cavalry, and four companies of artillery. This military was actively involved in the war of independence, but was beaten in several battles, including those of Yerbas Buenas, San Carlos, Quechereguas, Rancagua, Chacabuco and Maipú.

Following independence in 1816, the leaders of the United Provinces of the Rio de la Plata – a short-lived federation that had made up the Viceroyalty of the Rio de la Plata – realized their insecure position and decided to confront the supporters of the Spanish rule, the 'Royalists'. They established a combined, Argentinean-Chilean force, named the Army of the Andes, commanded by Bernardo O'Higgins and José de San Martin. This set out from San Juan in northern Argentina on 12 January 1817, crossed the Andes at Paso de Uspallata and Paso de los Patos, and took the Royalists entirely by surprise, defeating them at Chacabuco, near Santiago, a month later.

Following this success, the 5,000-strong Army of Chile (Ejército de Chile) was officially established in late 1817. This experienced several defeats against the Spaniards, early on, but won a sweeping final victory at Maipú, on 5 April 1818.[66]

Following its independence, Chile not only sought the best form of a government, but also a solid mix of defence capabilities. Despite austere economic situation, the country was able to recruit, organize, and fund the first navy squadron – which promptly participated in the liberation of Peru, in 1820.[67]

The triumph of the Conservatives against the Liberals during the Battle of Lircay – the final clash of the Chilean Civil War of 1829-1830 – signalled the start of a period of the conservative republic, during which Diego Portales – Chile's principal strongman in the period 1830-1837 – introduced profound changes in the military. The Army was increased in size to a total of three infantry battalions, two regiments of cavalry, a squadron of hussars, and an artillery regiment, and its commanders kept away from the politics.[68]

During the mid-19th Century, the Chilean Army became involved in the wars against the Peruvian-Bolivian Confederation and won the battle of Yungay, and subsequently contributed to the stability of the constitutional government. 1879, it fought the War of the Pacific against Peru and Bolivia again. This conflict stimulated the development of an important defence sector, responsible for keeping the military supplied, and inaugurated the colonisation of Chile's South.

Despite the victory, the War of the Pacific was important because

A group of youthful Chilean troops in the early 1970s. Other than the relatively modern FN-FAL assault rifles (seen on this photo), many of them were still armed with old Mauser Model 1912 and SIG SG 510 (also Sturmgewehr 57), and US-made M2 carbines. (Albert Grandolini Collection)

Chilean politicians and military officers realised the requirement for a professional military, supported by a well-developed logistic tail, security and health services. Therefore, the government of Domingo Santa Maria hired several Prussian officers as instructors. These were headed by Captain Emilio Körner, who also went on to serve as Deputy Director of the newly-established Military School.[69]

The Civil War of 1891 thus caught the Chilean military in the middle of major reforms – and it split into several factions. The Navy, and part of the Army commanded by Körner, sided with a group of parliamentarians that organized an uprising against the government of President Balmaceda, who promoted nationalist interests against those of foreign companies. However, most of the military remained loyal to the president, but Balmaceda lost the war and committed suicide.

German instructors remained important following this conflict too. They helped establish several military-education facilities, including the School for Non-Commissioned Officers (Escuela de Suboficiales y Clases), and encouraged cooperation with several other militaries in Latin America, which earned Chileans much prestige. By 1905, the Chilean Army – meanwhile reinforced by the National Guard – grew to about 150,000. The German mission remained in the country until 1914, when the reorganisation was considered complete.[70]

Despite its generally professional attitude, the Chilean military could not avoid involvement in subsequent political unrest, and its elements became involved in several mutinies and coup attempts. Nevertheless, it continued receiving sufficient funding for further growth and modernisation. Correspondingly, the Carabineros de Chile were established in 1927, and an air force (the Fuerza Aérea de Chile, FACh) was created from flying units of the army and the navy, three years later. The permanent position of the Commander-in-Chief of the Armed Forces was established in 1931.[71]

During the 1940s and 1950s, the Army established close cooperation with the military of the USA and began acquiring some armoured vehicles, followed by the introduction of a telecommunications branch, the Mountain School, and the Civil Defence to its structure. Changes during the 1960s were relatively minor, except with regards to the introduction of compulsory service for all able-bodied men between 20 and 45, and in regards of training, which was meanwhile provided by a permanently assigned US military mission, members of which also taught at the newly-established War Academy.

Thus, as of 1973, the Chilean Armed Forces totalled about 60,000 well-trained and disciplined officers and other ranks, although these were equipped with largely obsolete weapons. About 38,000 of these were assigned to the Army, which was organized into 6 infantry brigades, 2 armoured regiments, 2 motorised cavalry regiments, 4 cavalry regiments (3 of these mounted, and 1 de-facto an airborne regiment supported by helicopters), 8 artillery regiments, and an unknown number of anti-aircraft artillery battalions. Armour included a few old M4 Shermans and M3 Stuarts, twenty M24 Chafees and sixty M41 Walker Bulldogs, plus a small number of M113 armoured personnel carriers (APCs). The artillery component included 105mm towed pieces and some anti-tank guns, while anti-aircraft artillery consisted of World-War-II-era 20mm and 40mm pieces and was partially subjected to the control of the air force. The Army possessed relatively few of its own helicopters and thus remained dependent on FACh to transport its troops and supplies.[72]

The Chilean Navy of 1973 had a total of 18,000 officers and other ranks, and included a small Marine Corps. Other than warships – including two *Brooklyn*-class cruisers and another cruiser of Swedish origin bought in 1971, two *Fletcher*-class destroyers, four escort destroyers, two *Balao*-class submarines, four torpedo boats and various support ships, organized into a 'war squadron' – the Navy included a small unit of naval aviation (flying a miscellany of PBY-5A and HU-16A amphibians, and four Bell 206A Jet Ranger helicopters) and another of naval engineers. The Chilean Navy's officers were heirs of the tradition of the Royal Navy, and its commanders considered the 'military aristocracy' of the country. In 1973, the Navy ordered two *Leander*-class frigates and two *Oberon*-class attack submarines from Great Britain.[73]

A carabinero on the streets of Santiago: Carabineros were the main armed public force in Chile. (Albert Grandolini Collection)

In addition to these two regular military services, para-military and national security forces existed in form of the Carabineros (founded in April 1927). Equipped with personal firearms, but also eight Mowag MR.8 APCs, the Carabineros totalled about 28,000 troops deployed in no less than 17,000 bases around the country. As such, they were the only armed body present in all the communes around the country and living in direct contact with the civilian population.[74]

Table 1: Major Units of the Chilean Army, September 1973

Unit	Base
Ejercito de Chile **C-in-C: Major-General Augusto Pinochet**	
1st Infantry Regiment "Buin"	Santiago
2nd Infantry Regiment "Maipo"	Valparaiso
3rd Infantry Regiment "Yungay"	Los Andes
4th Infantry Regiment "Rancagua"	Arica
6th Infantry Regiment "Chacabuco"	Concepcion
8th Infantry Regiment "Tucapel"	Temuco
10th Infantry Regiment "Pudeto"	Punta Arenas
14th Infantry Regiment "Caupolicán"	Parvenir
16th Infantry Regiment "Talca"	Talca
18th Infantry Regiment "Guardia Vieja"	Los Andes
19th Infantry Regiment "Colchagua"	San Fernando
21st Infantry Regiment "Arica"	La Serena
22nd Infantry Regiment "Lautaro"	Rancagua
3rd Mountain Infantry Regiment "Los Ángeles"	Los Ángeles
2nd Armoured Regiment	Santiago
5th Cavalry Regiment "Lanceros"	Puerto Natales
1st Artillery Regiment "Tacna"	Santiago

Embattled and Entrenched Military

The Chilean military had actively participated in the formation of the nation throughout the 19th Century, and was crucial for its

As of the early 1970s, the Chilean Army was still operating at least a company worth of M3A1 Stuart light tanks, acquired from the USA during World War II. (Albert Grandolini Collection)

ability to expand and consolidate control over additional territories. Subsequently, the military was important in securing the vast and resource-rich nation. The modernisation resulted in an early definition of its 'corporate identity': influence of German instructors also meant that it was expected to play a central role in the further development of Chile. This thought was supported by the emergence of the concept of a 'total war', which advocated a mobilisation of all available forces in the case of another conflict – around the nucleus formed by the army. Eventually, a self-image was created of a strong, unified military as the centrepiece of Chile.[75]

However, similar aspirations in regards of a solid economic sector were shattered time and again. The harsh reality was that Chile remained a socially and economically backward country without major industry, in which social conflicts left the elite without a choice but to assign the military a repressive mission. This, in turn, created rifts within the Chilean military, large segments of which were curious to continue the modernisation, and industrialisation in particular.[76] Thus, time and again, the military did become involved in the politics, and often showed better skills in applying reforms than civilian politicians did. Unsurprisingly, the army remained – more or less – directly involved in the government until the return of civil rule, in 1932.[77]

By then, the power and influence of the military were profoundly weakened, despite social reforms it promoted in the 1920s. Defeated, the army abandoned its aspirations to power, and subjected itself to the rule of civilian governments that maintained it in a poorly-funded condition, isolated, and ignored by the political elite.[78]

The World War II, the US influence, and the Chile signing several multi-national defence treaties, prompted a reverse of this situation. US military missions were deployed at Valparaíso (in support of the Navy), El Bosque (in support of the air force), and in Santiago (in support of the Army and the Ministry of Defence), and had two objectives: to ensure the cooperation in the case of a major conflict with the USSR, and to ensure internal security – in the 'anti-communist' sense.[79]

Officers of the Chilean Navy. As it turned out, the Navy formed the heart of the militant opposition to Allende. (Albert Grandolini Collection)

The reforms prompted by US advisors brought the Chilean military out of its isolation and assigned it a new mission: the defence of the West against internal and external enemies. Their anti-communist ideology also endowed the Chilean military with new doctrinal ideas with regards to national security – which in turn had become a motive for greater participation in domestic affairs. Initially, civilian elites continued to ignore military institutions, although they were influenced by the Cold War paradigm too. For example, President González Videla quickly got rid of communists from the centre-left coalition that helped him form the government in 1946. He also did nothing when Admiral Jose Consiglio provided the US military advisers with a list of communist and trade-union activists in Valparaíso, shortly before repression of the same began in 1948.[80]

Following the Cuban revolution, but especially while facing a possible electoral victory of the left in the 1964 elections, Washington began providing for up to 10% of the Chilean defence budget, plus other aid packages. The result was a significant build-up of the military to a point where they not only began placing orders for modern weapons, like fighter jets (see sub-chapter on the Chilean air force below), but also grew in numbers. By the mid-1960s, it had 46,000 soldiers and 24,000 police officers, or 6-7 men per 1,000 inhabitants. With this, Chile was the most militarised country in Latin America – right after Cuba. As well as participating in international exercises, the Chilean military received training in counter-insurgency (COIN) operations, had about 2,600 of its officers and other ranks trained in the USA, and some 500 in Panama.[81]

This assistance came at some price. By adopting an inter-American alliance, the Chilean military leadership transferred its responsibility to US agencies; it had to be content with a limited sovereignty over some of the armament provided (this could be 'borrowed' by the US military if necessary); and US military intelligence began probing political views of Chilean military officers.[82]

The result was a continually increasing gap between the pluralist Chilean political scene and the military. For all practical purposes, there was an outright 'divorce' between the military and civilians, based on intense frustration and resentment of military officers towards political elites, aggravated by bad economic conditions.[83]

The first visible and dramatic manifestation of this breach came in 1968, when all the students of the War Academy Promotion submitted individual letters of resignation, citing difficulties in their professional and economic conditions. This event provoked the dismissal of the Minister of Defense and the C-in-C. Discontent continued the following year, when one of the top military officers, Major-General

The first group of US advisors assigned to the FACh, seen during their visit to one of local air bases in 1941. (Albert Grandolini Collection)

Viaux, rebelled as the head of the Tacna Regiment – one of the principal military units in Santiago. The underlying message of this act, widely shared among the ranks, was the demand that the military became the central institution of national security. Instead, the negotiations resulted in Viaux's surrender and retirement.[84]

Unsurprisingly, when Allende became president, he inherited a deeply entrenched military, which was convinced of having to fight another battle of the Cold War.

A row of Italian-made Breda Ba.65 light bombers of the FACh, as seen in the late 1930s. (Albert Grandolini Collection)

Fuerza Aérea de Chile

The history of military flying in Chile dates back to 1910, when the Chilean government instructed General Aristides Pinto to investigate the possibilities of establishing a flying school and a national military aviation service.[85] Following three years of planning, a flying school was established at the airfield of Lo Espejo under the direction of Captain Mauel Avalos Prado, who had been taught to fly at the Blériot School in Etampes. The first aircraft obtained were three Blériots; these were soon supplemented by three additional aircraft of the same origin, and three Sanchez-Besa, a Voisin, and Deperdussin. The first two Chilean military pilots obtained their flying certificates on 9 August 1913.

On 1 January 1915, the Chilean Military Aviation Service held the first ever flying display in Latin America, at El Bosque, in which eleven pilots and fourteen aircraft participated. By April 1914, the service was organized into two squadrons, each possessing five aircraft. Further reinforcements were acquired in 1917, in the form of six Bristol M.1Cs. It was in one of these that Lieutenant Dagoberto Godoy made the first aerial crossing of the Andes, on 12 December 1918.

A year later, the Department of Aviation was formed to administer military aviation in Chile, the National Aircraft Factory (Fabrica Nacional de Aeronaves) was founded in Santiago, and the nucleus of a Naval Aviation Service came into being, equipped with several floatplanes.

Following the slow growth of army and naval flying services during the 1920s, the FACh was officially established on 21 March 1930, by which time a number of additional air bases were constructed around the country, including Los Cóndores (Iquique), Maquehua (Temuco), and the seaplane bases of Chamiza (Puerto Montt) and Magalanes. Subsequently, fighter, bomber and general purpose units were deployed at El Bosque, Los Cóndores, and Maquehua, and equipped

Republic P-47D Thunderbolt formed the backbone of FACh's combat units of the 1940s and early 1950s. (Albert Grandolini Collection)

with a miscellany of Vickers Wibault and Curtis Hawk III single-seat fighters, Dornier Merkur L and Junkers R-42 bombers, and Vickers Vixen, Curtiss Falcon, and Junkers A-20 utility aircraft. The flying school at El Bosque used Avro 504-0s and de Havilland Gipsy Moth trainers, while the personnel strength grew to 80 officers and 1,500 other ranks. Further development of the FACh stagnated during the 1930s, although small numbers of aircraft were acquired from Germany and Italy.

In 1941, an advisory and training mission from the US military was deployed in Chile. The FACh was subsequently re-organized along the lines of the US Army Air Force, and received no fewer than 231 aircraft under the Lend-Lease program, including Fairchild PT-19 primary trainers, North American AT-6 and Vultee BT-13 advanced trainers, Sikorsky OS2U-3 reconnaissance floatplanes, Consolidated PBY-5A Catalina amphibians, Curtiss P-40 fighters, and Douglas

The second most-important combat type introduced to service during the World War II was the B-25 Mitchell light bomber. (Albert Grandolini Collection)

A flight of FACh's AT-6 advanced trainers, as seen in the 1950s. (Albert Grandolini Collection)

A-24 light bombers. By 1945, the air force was organized into four brigades based at Antofagasta, El Bosque, Temuco, and Punta Arenas, and was further strengthened through addition of Republic P-47D Thunderbolt fighter-bombers and North American B-25 Mitchell bombers.

The Americans withdrew after World War II, and the FACh did not purchase additional aircraft for years afterwards.

The Air Force's Growth of the 1960s

A major modernisation program was launched in 1952, when Chile placed orders for 17 additional P-47Ds, 36 Beech Model 45 Mentor primary trainers, and five de Havilland DHC-3 Otter utility transports abroad. Furthermore, 50 Fanaero-Chile Chincol primary trainers were designed and assembled at the Central Workshops at Rancagua. At least as important, is that it was during this period that the FACh entered the jet age: five de Havilland Vampire T.Mk 55s were ordered on 22 October 1953. These reached Chile in January 1954, were assembled and test-flown at El Cerillos Air Base (AB), and handed over to the air force between April and June of the same year. Further jets were acquired in the form of four Lockheed T-33-1-LO armed trainers, starting in October 1956. In 1959, Chile acquired nine additional T-33As, and a pair of reconnaissance-configured RT-33As, after which this type was transferred to Gropo 9, then based at El Tepual. In 1967, the surviving T-33As were reconfigured to

The first Chilean jet, the Vampire T.Mk 55 with serial J-01 (later J-301), delivered in 1954. (Albert Grandolini Collection)

Except for F-80s, Chile acquired 13 refurbished T-33As and 2 RT-33As, in 1956-1959 period. This photograph is one of the former, after it was converted to AT-33A standard in the late 1960s. (Albert Grandolini Collection)

In addition to the T-33As, Chile acquired 18 overhauled F-80C Shooting Star, single-seat fighter bombers, in 1957-1958. As of 1973, these served with the newly-established Grupo 12 in the south of the country. (via Santiago Rivas)

AT-33A standard and – together with both RT-33As – re-assigned to the Grupo 12, based at Punta Arenas. This unit was assigned the responsibility for air defence and ground attack in the south of the country.[86]

Meanwhile, remaining P-47s were replaced by 18 refurbished, ex-US Air Force (USAF) Lockheed F-80C-10-LO Shooting Star fighter jets, delivered between December 1957 and June 1958. These served with Los Cerillos-based Grupo 7 until 1964, when 15 survivors were grouped with AT-33As and RT-33As into the newly-established Grupo 12. Similarly, the bomber fleet – comprised of eight surviving

For most of the 1950s, 1960s and well into the 1970s, FACh's fleet of transport aircraft was dominated by Douglas C-47s. (Albert Grandolini Collection)

B-25Js, six Beech AT-11s, a Beech C-45, and a North American T-6 – was reinforced through addition of 4 Douglas B-26B and 34 B-26C Invaders, delivered between November 1954 and March 1958.[87] By then, the FACh totalled about 200 aircraft and 370 qualified pilots (of which about 150 were active), and 4,700 other personnel based at El Bosque, Antofagasta, Cerillos and Chabunco.[88]

The air force was re-equipped again during the 1960s. Vampire T.Mk 11s were overhauled and pressed into service as ground-attack fighters in 1961. They remained operational for the next ten years, by when structural life restrictions grounded all but one (J-301, ex-J-304). As replacements, in 1972 the FACh acquired four ex-RAF Vampire T.Mk 11s (including registrations WZ512, XD614, XE857, and XJ774), and then six ex-Fleet Air Arm Sea Vampire T.Mk 22s (XA107, XA128, XA166, XG769, XG772, and XG777).[89]

Meanwhile, in 1964, supported by US military aid, the Chilean government commenced negotiations for the acquisition of modern fighter-bombers. Following protracted negotiations, the Hawker Hunter emerged victorious in 1966, and the FACh placed an order for 15 overhauled aircraft (Contract No. HSA/66/C/066) brought to FGA.Mk 9 standard, as Hunter F.Mk 71. Deliveries of this batch were completed by June 1968, by when three of the airframes in question were converted to FR.Mk 10 standard (resulting in the variant officially designated the Hunter FR.Mk 71A), for reconnaissance purposes. A follow-up order (Contract No. 69/C/084) was placed in 1969, stipulating deliveries of nine additional Hunters by 1971, while a third order – including three Hunter FR.Mk 71As – was completed by January 1974. Finally, Chile placed two orders for a total of five Hunter T.Mk 72 two-seat conversion trainers. In all, the FACh thus acquired a total of 39 Hunters of four different sub-variants.[90]

By 1973, the FACh comprised about 10,000 officers and other ranks, and operated about 50 combat aircraft. Except for a total of 32 Hunters and 10 Vampires, the primary types still in service were some 10 remaining Douglas B-26 Invaders, eight Grumman HU-16C Albatross and three PBY-5A Catalina amphibians. The transport component of the FACh totalled two Lockheed C-130 Hercules, eight de Havilland DHC-6 Twin Otter, and a miscellany of older Douglas DC-3 and C-47s. While Beech Model 45 still served as primary trainers, the air force also operated four Bell UH-1 Iroquois utility helicopters.[91]

Table 2: Order of Battle of the Fuerza Aérea de Chile, September 1973

Unit	Equipment	Base
Comando de Unidades Aéreas, HQ Santiago C-in-C: Air General Gustavo Leigh Guzman		
Grupo 1	AT-6	Los Cóndores (Iquique)
Grupo 10	DHC-2, C-47, C-130	Los Cerrillos (Santiago)
I Brigada Aérea		Cerro Moreno/Ala Base 1 (Antofagasta)
Grupo 5	DHC-2, DHC-3, S-55	La Chamiza (Puerto Montt)
Grupo 7	Hunter F.Mk 71/71A & FR.Mk 72	Cerro Moreno
Grupo 8	B-26C, Vampire T.Mk 11/22	Cerro Moreno
Grupo 9	F-80C, T-33A, Hunter F.Mk 71/71A	La Chamiza
Escuadrilla de Enlace 11	C-47	Cerro Moreno
Bateria de Artilleria No.3		Cerro Moreno
II Brigada Aérea		El Bosque
Grupo 2	PBY-5, HU-16B, S-55	Quintero (Valparaíso)
Escuadrilla de Enlace 12	C-47	Quintero
III Brigada Aérea		Maquehue (Temuco)
Grupo 3	AT-6, BT-13	Maquehue
IV Brigada Aérea		Magellanes (Punta Arenas)
Grupo 6	C-47	Magellanes
Escuadrilla de Enlace 13	C-47	Magellanes
Grupo de Artilleria No.4		Magellanes

Initially serialled J-01 to J-05, FACh's Vampire T.Mk 55s were re-numbered to J-301 to J-305 in the 1960s. The example visible in the rear is J-304 – which was the first to receive a camouflage pattern (in grey and dark green). (Albert Grandolini Collection)

Chile's extensive coast necessitated the maintenance of a sizeable fleet of amphibious aircraft, deployed as much for maritime patrol as for search and rescue duties. Grumman HU-16B Albatross – including this example – were acquired in order to replace old Consolidated PBY-5s, in the 1960s. (Albert Grandolini Collection)

The first group of Chilean pilots that converted to Hunter F.Mk 71s, with one of their mounts. Notable is the unit insignia of the Grupo 7 applied below the cockpit of the fighter-bomber in the rear. (FACh via Oscar Ruf Willson)

Allende's Policy Towards the Armed Forces

Allende's policy towards the Chilean military was characterized by his desire to strengthen the national character and to break ties with the USA, and the president's idea that through insistent respect for the Constitution and the rule of law, he could motivate the military to follow in fashion.[92]

Seriously concerned about the military's preparedness to obey the orders of a Marxist government, Allende and his aides went to great extent in their efforts to appease top generals and distance them from US advisors. After his ratification as President by the Congress, Allende confirmed Major-General Carlos Prats as the C-in-C, and took care to strictly respect the military hierarchy and protocols. Moreover, he responded favourably to the military's demands for modern armament. Therefore, new warships were ordered in Great Britain; negotiations were opened for the acquisition of Northrop F-5E Tiger II fighters from the USA; and a project for development of nuclear energy was assigned to the Army. Throughout the years of his presidency, Allende also continued increasing the defence budget.[93]

Nevertheless, the 'military problem' continued to occupy a central place in the president's struggle for the defence of constitutional order.

A row of Hunter F.Mk 71/71As as seen while in service with Grupo 7, at Cerro Moreno AB, outside Antofagasta, in the early 1970s. (Albert Grandolini Collection)

Allende (right) with Major-General Augusto Pinochet, commander of the Chilean Army. Allende's belief that his own insistence upon the constitutional order, might be followed by the military proved his biggest mistake. (Albert Grandolini Collection)

Between 5 September and 24 October 1970, Allende spent plenty of time trying to find a common language with the military, and convince top generals to support his program. Still shocked by Schneider's assassination, military commanders decided to respect the popular will expressed during the elections. In this regard it can be said that Schneider's death at the hands of a right-wing extremist traumatized the Chilean military to a degree where it maintained neutrality for the next two years.[94]

For much of this period, the Chilean president strongly promoted an integration of military officers into the UP's government – which was perfectly in line of his idea of involving the military in the economic and social development of the country. Correspondingly, he appointed generals as ministers of transport, distribution, nuclear energy research and other vital sectors. Other officers were appointed to the management of public companies: General Pedro Palacios at the Chuquicamata mine; Colonel Claudio Sepúlveda to that of El Teniente; Colonel Sergio Nuño headed the nationalized chemical industry Du Pont (producer of explosives), and General Orlando Urbina was appointed Vice-Chairman of the Commission in charge of organizing the Conference on United Nations Trade and Development (UNCTAD III) in Santiago of April 1972. Allende thus had the military involved in the recovery of national wealth and the conquest for economic independence from imperialism.

While foremost concentrating on higher commanders, Allende didn't neglect the other ranks. Mid- and low-ranking officers were granted economic and professional improvements, and – in June 1973 – the government took care that all soldiers to receive the right to vote (hitherto confined to the officers only).[95]

This policy proved effective: despite countless offers from the Right, the military did not respond to any of the solicitations. On the contrary: relations between Allende's government and the High Command of the Chilean military remained good, and the majority of officers and other ranks – no matter how fiercely anti-Communist – repeatedly expressed their opposition to any kind of a coup.

This began to change only in September 1972, when the first supposed coup plot was discovered. This aimed to create unrest through a blockade of communications and a paralysis of the economy, after which there would be an attack on soldiers during the parade commemorating the National Day. Although no precise details about instigators or their relations to the military were ever released, the denunciation of the plot coincided with the retirement of General Alfredo Canales, implicated in inciting a rebellion of naval officers. If the military connections of that plot were neutralized, the civilian were not: this became obvious during the month-long strike staged by the Right with US support, in October 1972. Although acting reluctantly, the military contributed to the return to order, and then had a number of its top officers appointed ministers in the government. Thus, the military became directly involved in politics – and this on Allende's initiative. Ironically, the president and his cabinet considered this act unavoidable, for they were convinced that the revolutionary process had reached a stage at which it became impossible for the military to remain neutral – even at the price of causing a deep rift between various members of the UP coalition, some of which continued to propagate the organisation of workers and peasants into a 'popular army'. Although not intended, this exposed the military to persistent attacks from the Left and the Right, causing discontent and then political divisions within its ranks. As officers became actors in a strongly ideologised political struggle, discipline and obedience to the civil power began to deteriorate, too.

Military Wings of the PS

Nominally, the defence of the constitutional government was the responsibility of the state security apparatus. However, various members of the UP coalition not only criticised Allende for his 'disarmed revolution', but began creating their own militias to protect the government.[96]

This was another irony of the situation, because the majority of contemporary Chilean political parties were entirely disinterested in military affairs. This was rather unsurprising considering that two thirds of the population were living in urban centres, and Chile was the most industrialised country in Latin America. Furthermore, its left-wing movements had participated in a relatively stable democracy for decades, and even the PCCh and the PS were traditionally committed to peaceful means of achieving power. Finally, arid deserts in the north and Patagonia in the south, with their climate extremes, and the geographic isolation from the rest of the World, made Chile ill-suited for launching armed insurgencies.

This did not mean that no related attempts were undertaken. After Ernesto Che Guevara created the Military of National Liberation (Ejercito de Liberacion nacional, ELN) – an international political-military organisation designed to spread insurgency into southern Latin America – he paid special attention to Chile. For Che, the country was the only place where socialism could rise to power through elections, and thus it had to serve for channelling logistical support for the guerrilla active elsewhere, foremost in Bolivia. Thus, in the mid-1960s, he established the Chilean Section of the ELN, members of which received military training in Cuba. Their leader, Elmo Catalán, joined the Front of the Americas (headed by Manuel Piñeiro) and received the task of setting up a clandestine political and military apparatus with help of local activists.

Over time, about 100 Chileans became involved in the ELN – the majority of whom were members of the PS (within which they formed a powerful faction) – of which about 20 were trained in use of light arms in Cuba. Their network began sending arms and medicaments to Che's guerrillas in Bolivia, and – after Che's death in October 1967 – helped extract Cuban survivors to Tahiti. Subsequently, some Chileans participated in the Teoponte operations led by the Bolivian

As of early 1970s, Chile was one of the most industrialised nations in Latin America, and one of only a few that had the majority of its population living in cities. This view is of downtown Santiago from that period of time. (Mark Lepko Collection)

guerrillas – that ended in a quick disaster.[97]

In early 1968, some of the cadre trained in Cuba, and several peasant leaders, founded the Organa – a clandestine political and military organisation set to prepare an armed struggle. The Organa and the Chilean ELN merged in late 1969, but then decided to support Allende's candidacy for the elections.[98] Convinced that the USA and the Chilean Right would try to overthrow the new government, the militants began organising training camps around the country – including those like the Guayacán Urban Guerrilla School (outside Santiago), and the Chaihuin Rural Guerrilla School (south of Valdivia).[99] The build-up of the PS military wing experienced a further impetus following the Congress of Serena, in January 1971, when many of ELN's cadre were elected into the highest instances of that party. Led by Arnoldo Camú, member of the PS leadership, they established a Defence Committee divided into five task-forces:

- Presidential Security Apparatus (GAP, led by Domingo Blanco and Jaime Sótelo)
- Intelligence and Counter-Intelligence Unit (led by Ricardo Pincheira Núñez)
- Operational Task Forces (*Grupos Especiales Operativos*, GEOs),
- Agitation and Propaganda Squadron (AGP), and
- Military Relations Group (EMA, responsible for activities within the Chilean military).

Furthermore, they set up the National Centre for Public Opinion (CENOP), consisting of sociologists, psychologists, and other young professionals of confidence, responsible for preparing means of communications and manuals for local organisations in the field.[100]

The PS military wing was poorly armed. Only the members of the industrial belt group in San Joaquin had about 120 AK-47s and five rocket launchers, while the rest was largely unarmed. Furthermore, members of this body became strongly divided between supporters of peaceful and militant means of the revolution. Arguing that the military apparatus proved obedient to Allende, even some of former ELN members began supporting the moderates. Correspondingly, the activities of the PS military wing remained limited to the protection of Allende and his 'Chilean Way into Socialism' – even though the group continued sending its activists to Cuba for training all through 1971-1973.[101]

Aware of Allende's determination not to leave the La Moneda Palace in the case of an emergency, the PS military wing was forced to abandon the idea of evacuating the president to some safe refuge from where he could direct an armed struggle. Instead, it developed a plan for the defence of La Moneda in the form of defence lines stretching in concentric circles around this part of Santiago, and with support of masses of supporters organized by GEO's activists. The first circle of this defence perimeter was to be established in public buildings adjacent to the palace; the second was to run through the premises of the UP Party, and the third was to be formed by the industrial belt squadrons, where workers and students were expected to block any kind of rebel forces, in combination with loyal soldiers. The two inboard defence lines were to be supported by snipers of the GAP and the PS.[102]

The planning for emergencies envisaged further operations on the periphery of Santiago de Chile, too. For example, in the north, communal commands of Renca and Conchali were to contain the Buin Regiment of the Army, and block access to San Felipe and Los Andes Districts. Communal commands of San Bernardo and Vicuña Mackenna received the task of isolating the Pirque and the Ferrocarrileros Regiments in the south. In the south-west, the communal command of San Joaquin was to block the San Bernardo Infantry School and the El Bosque AB. To the west, the communal command of Cerrillos was to block the Cerrillos AB and control the access routes to the capital. Following a period of 'containment', all the forces in question were to capture arsenals of arms, and arm the workers.

However, this plan was not yet in place and was known only to a very small group of leftist leaders within the Defence Committee as of 11 September 1973.[103] Actually, at the time, only a small number of ex-ELN militants were mobilised – and these were deployed to Chuquicamata, with the task of protecting the mines from possible attacks by far-right extremists, and securing loyalty of the Calama Infantry Regiment. Other leading activists of the PS military wing were scattered all over the country, and busy organising defences of various communal commands.[104] The principal reason for this situation was that the military wing of the PS never attracted very much popular support. As a consequence, a very small group of ill-armed and poorly-trained militants – as brave as they were – was all that stood between Allende and the military as of 11 September 1973.

Military Wings of Other Leftist Parties

The Defence Committee of the PS attracted most of the attention of the Chilean military and convinced it that the leftists were operating a strong military wing. Actually, for reasons described above, the related discussion created a fake reality and backfired not only upon the Left, but the government too – foremost through the defeat of pluralists within the military.

Attempts by other Chilean leftist parties to organize their military wings thus largely escaped attention. The PCCh, for example, had already launched related efforts in 1963, when its Commission of Vigilance (Comisiones de vigilancia) was established. Over time, this included 10 top commanders and several 'groups of young boys' (grupos chicos), totalling about 200 well-prepared, even if poorly armed militants. According to the later report by Lúis Corvalán, the PCCh possessed an 'arsenal' of about 400 assault rifles and 6 grenade launchers (with 3 spare projectiles each) – but never undertook any serious politico-military training.[105] On the contrary, Volodia Teitelboim stresses that the PCCh had thousands of members with basic knowledge about guerrilla tactics as of 1973, of which about 2,000 were trained on arms, in self-defence, and urban guerrilla warfare.

Starting in 1965, the MIR developed its own military wing, too. This consisted of various left-wingers hostile to the legalism and traditional leftist parties, who propagated a popular armed insurrection as the only way to overthrow the capitalist system. Indeed, one of the most important theoretical and strategic contributions by the MIR to revolutionary thought in Chile was the introduction of armed struggle forms as a strategy to face the state and the ruling classes.

Led by Miguel Enríquez, the MIR was completely reorganized in 1967, when Politico-Military Groups (Grupos Politico-Militares, GPMs) came into being with the aim of providing intermediate organisational infrastructure. Henceforth, the party pursued a rigorous recruiting policy, custom-tailored to armed action. Through robberies in particular, the MIR aimed to establish a link between material conditions of workers and investment into its own structures.[106] When confronted with repression run by the Carabineros, this movement went into hiding. Moreover, once the MIR was informed about Allende's candidacy for elections, it suspended militant activity.

Ironically, this party still refused to participate in the campaign, arguing that, '...an electoral victory does not mean the end of the conquest of the power by the workers.'[107] On the contrary, after Allende's victory, it exercised self-criticism and concluded that, '...the electoral victory of the left is a huge step forward in the struggle of the people for the conquest of power.'[108]

That was not the end of such contradictions. While the MIR subsequently retained its organisational independence, and its general vision of the revolutionary transformation, and continued demanding for violent destruction of the 'bourgeois state', it also decided to 'critically support' the policies of the UP coalition, and strengthened its relations to several parties and the government. Indeed, following strikes of October 1972, it developed strong relationships to the industrial belts of Santiago, Valparaíso and Concepción. Nevertheless, the MIR has re-established its military wing too. Designated the Central Force (Fuerza central), and about 40 strong, this group received para-military training – sometimes at the same camps where GAP members were trained, too.[109]

The MIR was quite early in recognizing the threat of a military coup. Correspondingly, three of its leaders had drafted a 'strategic plan for political-military struggle against putschism' already by 1972. This was a hesitant mix of an occupation of urban areas, withdrawal to the countryside, and a guerrilla war along classic revolutionary principles – which was strongly dependent upon the idea of widespread popular support for Allende.[110]

Further planning was concluded in early July 1973, by when greater emphasis was put upon cooperation with the PS in Cerillos, and industrial belt groups in O'Higgins. However, such initiatives remained small in number and rather isolated, and resulted only in some self-defence training of a few activists. According to Tomás Inostroza, it was foremost the lack of suitable arms and ammunition that made the idea of an armed resistance to a military coup anything but hypothetical. Even the famous 'popular tanks' – sometimes cited in the international press – were little other than forklifts with steel plating attached, designed for defence of specific factories from attacks by far-right extremists.[111]

Overall, it can thus be concluded that most of leftist political leaders – even most of leaders of industrial belts – advocated calm, and relied on the loyalty of the military.

GAP: Grupo des Amigos Personales

Taking place in a climate of polarisation, the election campaign of 1970 prompted Allende's relatives, such as Osvaldo Puccio, Jaime Suárez, Augusto Olivares, and Eduardo Paredes, to establish their own, rudimentary protection services.[112] Most of them depended upon ex-ELN militants, such as Francisco Gómez, alias 'Fernando', former chief of security for Dariel Alarcón Ramírez, leader of the special unit of the Cuban Ministry of Interior, for advice. Fernando eventually found himself in charge of a small ELN cadre responsible for the protection of Allende, supervised by Beatriz Allende, Paredes, and Rolando Calderón, and reinforced by soldiers with special forces training, like Mario Melo, purged from the army because of their Marxist ideas.[113]

The attempted kidnapping and the death of Major-General Schneider prompted an expansion of this group into the Group of Personal Friends (Grupos de Amigos Personales, GAP), which totalled between 20 and 30 operatives armed with revolvers, pistols, shot-guns and Winchester rifles. They protected Allende's residence in Tomás Moro Street (acquired in February 1971), but were based in a house in El Cañaveral, which was also used for training. By 1973, the GAP counted more than 70 men, armed with about 100 AK-47s, 50 Walther PPK, Uzi and MP-40 submachineguns, RPG-7 launchers, and 60 Colt P-38 revolvers – all donated by Castro during his visit. They were organized into three sections:

- Escort section (20 armed men responsible for protection of the president, equipped with a radio, and driving Fiat cars that could reach a speed of 200km/h)
- Advance Section (responsible for security of all places visited by the president, and working in coordination with the Carabineros and the Police)
- Garrison Section (responsible for security of Allende's residence, the El Cañaveral training centre, and La Moneda palace).[114]

Thanks to an initiative by Beatriz Allende, all the members of the GAP were trained by advisors from the Cuban Ministries of Interior and the Armed Forces, in Chile, while an additional group was sent

President Allende during an official visit. All the men in civilian suits around his car were members of the GAP. (Albert Grandolini Collection)

for similar training Cuba in late 1972. Thanks to the Cuban support, the service was improved to a degree where during Castro's visit it directly cooperated with similar Cuban services, and distinguished itself for loyalty and professionalism.[115]

This gradual institutionalization of the GAP allowed the MIR to carry out a series of activities concealed under the 'protection of the President'. With 'help of Cuban officials', the party quickly set up several serious paramilitary formations, some based inside GAP's facility in El Cañaveral, while up to 1000 of its cadre received tactical training. This indicates that the GAP in this period was not only a device for the security of Allende, but also a training school for fighters, i.e. that it became a nucleus of a revolutionary army. However, if the activity of the MIR within the GAP strengthened its combat capability, it also increased the risks of infiltration and provocation within circles close to Allende. Indeed, certain actions by members of the GAP were used by the right-wing to denounce the president and question the purpose of the organisation. For example, in April 1972, following an ordinary car accident, the police discovered plans of military installations and several weapons on GAP members.[116]

Furthermore, in 1972, the PS decided that the GAP could not be left autonomous; that its members had to act professionally and behave irreproachably. Therefore, it took over the GAP, appointed Marcelo Schilling as liaison officer between it and the PS, and excluded all the members of the MIR from it. From that moment onwards, the group became solely responsible for personal protection of Allende, his family and residence.[117]

While remaining relatively small, the Group of Personal Friends represented an important and strategic part of the future military force the Defence Committee of the PS sought to develop.

Chilean leftists were slow in realising that a coup had been launched, and were desperately ill-prepared to deal with the military assault. They had no plan for a pre-emptive attack even in the event that they were informed in time, and only widely-exaggerated ideas about possible leftist forces ready to take over the control of the country in the case of an emergency. This was a direct result of all the leftist parties' rejection of serious consideration of an armed confrontation with their opponents – yet fully along their official slogan, 'No to Civil War!' While some of them did analyse the uprising of the Spanish military in July 1936, none came to the conclusion that all of the Chilean military might rebel, or that the population would be resigned to the defeat. Instead, they remained convinced that the military would not move – and that until the last moment. In September 1972, for example, the Soviet Ambassador to Chile, A. V. Basov, recorded the following details of a conversation with Volodia Teitelboim and Luis Corvalán:

- Volodia Tetielboim reports a chat with the head of the counter-intelligence of the Army, General Sepúlveda. There was an agreement on the coordination of the security forces and parties of the people's block...It was decided at the same time to mobilize forces loyal to the government... It is understood that to prevent and counterbalance a military coup... Corválan and Teitelboim have no doubts about the 'loyal altitude of the military command', the officer corps, and General Prats.[118]

Exactly a year later, only a few days before the coup of 11 September, the leadership of the PCCh stated that, '...the legality of the government is a force against the coup, as is the prevalence of professional spirit ... among the armed forces...'[119]

Thus a situation came into being where, as of September 1973, the Chilean Left was unprepared and de-facto unarmed, while those plotting to crush the Chilean democracy were firmly convinced that the coup they were about to unleash would be a matter of life and death.

CHAPTER 4

PLOTTING THE COUP

The military coup of 11 September 1973 was the result of the strategy initiated by elements within Chilean society opposed to the Allende policy. This strategy aimed to create economic and social tensions, and a climate of general disorder through acts of sabotage, terrorism, speculation, stoppages of production; and then blame of the government for provoking a rift within Chilean society, with the aim of destroying the economy and thus endangering national security – which ultimately should push for the intervention of the military.

The strategy in question was initiated by civilians in contact with the military, including a number of media owners, editorial writers for *El Mercurio*, and similar activists already involved in attacks on legal institutions and other insurrectionary activities.

The Cofradía Náutica del Pacífico Austral and the Civil Plot

The first group of civilians that favourised a military coup was the Naval Brotherhood of the Southern Pacific (*Cofradía Náutica del Pacífico Austral*), led by Edwards Eastman, with Admiral José Toribio Merino as deputy. Established in 1968, this brought together a number of senior naval officers – including Patricio Carvajal, Arturo Troncoso, Joseph Radic – and civilians, like Roberto Kelly (a retired captain with good contacts with the US intelligence services), Hernan Cubillos (former naval officer), and René Silva Espejo (who maintained links between the navy, the army and air force).[120]

Cofradía was an important nucleus of the conspiracy that prepared the coup. Its meetings took place during meals taken at the homes of the members, most often in Viña del Mar, and often saw the participation of US military advisers, like Lieutenant-Colonel Patrick Ryan (head of the US Naval Section in Valparaíso), or CIA-officers.[121] Before long, the original nucleus was reinforced through the inclusion of several economists from the Catholic University, and then by Generals Sergio Arellano and Arturo Yovane (the latter served with the Carabineros), who were to play a key role on 11 September 1973.

Next, the *Cofradía* sought to establish links with different employers' associations opposed to Allende, foremost the Confederation of Production and Trade, led by Jorge Fontaine, and the National Agricultural Company, headed by Benjamín Matte (owner of the agro-industrial company ULA).[122] The result of this effort was the Society for Manufacturing Advancement (*Sociedad de Fomento Fabril*, SOFOFA), which came into being in Viña del Mar in September 1971 and included additional businessmen. The SOFOFA played a crucial role in organising the strikes of October 1972 and July-August 1973, by which time its coordinating committees were staging weekly meetings in Cubillo's office of the Lord Cochrane Publishing House, to decide on further press campaigns against the Allende Government.[123]

The SOFOFA did not limit its activities to meetings and propaganda campaigns, but began steering the activities of such militant groups as the Homeland and Freedom (*Patria y Libertad*) movement. Founded during the second half of 1970 by lawyer Pablo Rodríguez Grez to oppose Allende, this was a nationalist, corporatist, and anti-communist movement that strongly opposed the UP. Its activists began appearing on the streets wearing helmets and carrying clubs and wooden spears, and used to wear a logo showing a spider with three links of a broken chain. While no more than 500 strong, they were well-organised into sections for 'men', 'women', 'youth', the 'front' and the 'invisible front' – and supported by a number of businessmen that avoided acting as official members of the organisation.[124]

Several times through early 1973, the situation in Chile deteriorated to the point where the military had to be deployed on the streets to prevent further violence. This M113 was deployed in Melipilla, south of Santiago, during a strike by truckers in November 1972. (Albert Grandolini Collection)

The End of the Constitutional Opposition

With its electoral success in March 1973 the government ended the participation of the military in power. But Allende reiterated his decision to accentuate the role of the FF. AA in the field of economy and development, to upgrade the role of the staff and coordinated the action of the government with the council of chief commanders. The role played by the military in the government was considered positive by the UP parties. Minister Prats, in particular, received general recognition for his management, including assuming the vice-presidency of the republic during Allende's trip abroad in late 1972, and he returned to his C-in-C with great political prestige.

In turn, this convinced the opposition that the only way to defeat the government was by force. The next step the Right initiated was its unification with the PDC, which was considered decisive because of its parliamentary weight and influence in the population. Correspondingly, the moderate leadership of this party was overthrown under pressure from Frei, in May 1973, in favour of numerous radicals. Officially, Frei adopted the strategy of constitutional confrontation with Allende, and of blocking all governmental projects. Simultaneously, he moved the PDC closer to the PN and Patria y Libertad, sealing an alliance between his party and the Right. This happened at a time Chile was entering what many considered a decisive phase – one that could end only with the capitulation of one of the opponents.

On 15 June 1973, the Right organized unrest in Santiago before a counteroffensive of workers mobilized by the CUT. Six days later, Allende's supporters concentrated in Santiago in a great demonstration of strength with the watchword of preventing civil war. Meanwhile, economic chaos was fostered through multiple terror attacks (most of these originating from within the ranks of retired naval officers), assaults on leftist protesters, and the creation of a workers' opposition to the government. In November 1972, a bomb was discovered in Admiral Huerta's garden. Admiral Merino took the opportunity to denounce the chaos and sought to find the terrorists within the ranks of extreme leftists. Culprits were found following a protracted investigation, in June 1973: all belonged to a group led by former naval officers linked to Huerta.[125]

The situation worsened even further when the government

presented its project of education reform: this triggered student protests that were publicly criticised by Rear Admiral Huerta in what became the first public appearance of concordance between the Right and the officers.

Although some officers began delivering incendiary speeches against the government by 1972, activism of the Right generally met little sympathy within the military. Knowing that it needed the military to defeat the government, the SOFAFA then launched a campaign accusing the officers of cowardice and support for a Marxist dictatorship.

The opposition was not confined to insurrectional mobilization: it established links with additional officers and began encouraging them to organize a mutiny. In November 1972, a group of civilians approached Admiral Merino to ask him when the Navy would rise. Merino assured them that the measures were taken and that the best time would be for Allende's tour abroad, starting on 6 December. Although that plot misfired, naval officers continued planning actions against the government. A crucial figure that crystallised during this period was Major-General Sergio Arellano Stark, who spent months meeting with other officers: for him, retention of the unity of the Chilean military was the essence of the entire enterprise. Reinforced by such as Javier Palacios, Sergio Nuño and Arturo Viveros, Stark proved successful to the point where all that was left to be done by September 1973, was to decapitate the high command – which remained loyal to Allende.[126]

The Tancazo Affair

A few days before 29 June 1973, a conspiracy against the civilian authorities was discovered by General Mario Sepúlveda, commander of the Santiago Garrison. He promptly informed his immediate superiors and José Tohá, Minister of Defence. The latter went public with this information, and all nine plotters were arrested shortly after, on 28 June.[127] However, early in the morning of the following day, a column of 16 armoured vehicles – including M113 APCs and several M41 tanks – and 80 soldiers drove out of the base of the 2nd Armoured Battalion in Santiago and moved in the direction of the downtown. Led by Colonel Roberto Souper, who had just learned that he would be relieved of command for his involvement in the conspiracy, the troops encircled La Moneda and the Ministry of Defence Building, just across the Plaza de la Libertad. Two minutes before 0900 hrs in the morning, the troops involved opened fire at these two symbols of the constitutional government.

Shortly after, one of the tanks made its way to the main entrance of the Ministry of Defence, drove up the steps, and opened fire directly through the doors. Small arms fire killed Sergeant Rafael Veillena from the 2nd Division when he looked out of a window in the 9th Floor, while other workers and employees ran away in panic. Outside, the mutineers shot of a woman who worked at the State Bank in Banderas Streets, and a couple at the corner of Moneda and Agustinas Streets.

Once again, it was Sepúlveda's intervention that saved the day. He called for support from the commander of the Military Institute, General Guillermo Pickering, and – together with Prats – developed a plan to neutralize Souper's mutineers. Prats acted without delay and began deploying loyalist units around the city. While receiving support from the Tacna Infantry Regiment, he overcame hesitant resistance from the Junior Officers School. Nevertheless, by 1030, several units joined the mission against Souper.[128]

Meanwhile, Allende was active too. At 0930 hrs, he addressed the nation via radio, announcing his unequivocal decision to defend the constitutional government, and calling upon the workers of Santiago to occupy the factories, and '...be ready in case it is necessary to

The so-called *Tancazo* began with Colonel Souper leading a column of M3s, M113s and M41s out of the base of the 2nd Armoured Battalion in direction of downtown Santiago, early in the morning of 29 June 1973. (Albert Grandolini Collection)

Troops commanded by Souper arriving in downtown Santiago in a M3 half-track. (Albert Grandolini Collection)

M41 tank leading a M3 APC, loaded with troops of the 2nd Armoured Battalion, down a major street in Santiago. (Albert Grandolini Collection)

fight along [with] the soldiers of Chile'. Similar calls were issued by the leaders of the UP, resulting in an occupation of 244 different companies during the day.[129]

Arriving at the corner of 18th Street and O'Higgins Avenue, Prats then left his car while carrying a Thompson submachine gun. After

Carabineros quickly deployed to protect La Moneda in response to Souper's coup attempt on 29 June 1973. This group arrived supported by a Mowag armoured car. (Albert Grandolini Collection)

José Toha, Minister of Interior, together with a group of troops in front of La Moneda, on 29 June 1973. (Albert Grandolini Collection

passing by a number of civilians that had congregated nearby, he met the troops led by Colonel Juilo Canessa, and ordered them to deploy their artillery pieces down the avenue, and point them at the mutineers. Then Prats took what he subsequently called 'a calculated risk', and walked over to Souper's positions, seeking an opportunity to talk with his troops and thus prevent any unnecessary bloodshed. According to Prats:

'I then decided to advance in the company of Lieutenant-Colonel Osvaldo Hernández, Captain Roger Vergara, and 1st Sergeant Omar Vergara. Extremely moved, Villaroel, the military chaplain, gave us the last absolution'.[130]

At around 1110 hrs, the three officers reached the corner of Alameda and Teatinos Streets, where they stopped only steps away from a tank. The commander of the later trained his machine gun on the group, but did not open fire. Prats ordered him to come out and identify himself, to obey his orders, and to surrender to the troops of the Junior Officers School. According to the account of a journalist watching the events nearby:

'...the soldier came down, stood at attention before the general, and saluted. That tank would not fire again at the Ministry of Defence or La Moneda that morning.'[131]

Encouraged, Prats then went on from tank to tank, and the crews of other combat vehicles, located south of the palace.[132] Some crews fled rather than surrender. However, once the reinforcements from

Two M41s moving in direction of La Moneda, to protect the palace from coup-plotters involved in Tancazo. (Albert Grandolini Collection)

The coup plot of Colonel Souper prompted a significant reaction from the Chilean military: as well as two M41s, several companies of troops were deployed in front of the presidential palace. (Albert Grandolini Collection)

the 1st Infantry Regiment in Buin – led by nobody less than Major-General Augusto Pinochet – arrived on the scene, the mutineers gave up. The last to give up was a unit deployed north of La Moneda.

Prats then walked inside and ordered the GAP to search the palace and nearby buildings, before being joined by General Pickering – who meanwhile cleared the mutineers from the western side of the palace – and Minister Tohá. Overall, the shooting at La Moneda ceased by 1130, and the coup appeared to be over.[133]

Souper surrendered latter the same day, after units of the Tacna Regiment besieged and opened fire upon the base of the 2nd Battalion, where he had taken refuge. In the evening, Allende addressed a massive demonstration staged in support of the government, in front of La Moneda. Before long, it was discovered that the instigators of the coup attempt were the principal leaders of the Patria y Libertad movement – who sought asylum in the Ecuadorian embassy.[134] A year later, they admitted that the involvement of other units was planned, but that Prat's quick intervention prevented these from taking part. This made it clear that without the support of the High Command of the military, probably without an elimination of Prats too, no coup would ever be possible.[135]

For civilians, the brutality with which the military mutineers treated the civilian population – characterised by the film shot by a Swedish journalist who filmed his own assassination – should have provided a stark warning about what would happen starting with 11 September 1973. Tragically, this was not the case.[136]

Soldiers loyal to president Allende call upon the mutineers to abort the attempted coup of 29 June 1973. (Albert Grandolini Collection)

Resumption of Protesting

After a declaration of timid disapproval of the coup by the PDC, all the opposition tried to minimize and even justify the *Tancazo*. For their part, Eduardo Frei, President of the Senate, his colleague Luis Pareto, President of the Chamber of Deputies and the Supreme Court didn't condemn it. Thus, for the alleged defenders of the Constitution, democracy and the rule of law, the coup attempt didn't give rise to republican proclamations, but to the confirmation of a guilty complicity of the opposition. The request of the Government to the Congress to declare a state of siege, in order to facilitate the search of the culprits and the seditious ramifications, was rejected by the opposition[137].

The Right resumed its strategy of October 1972 by organizing a truckers' strike while a wave of terrorist attacks shook the country and caused chaos. Shortly before, on 13 July, the leader of *Patria y Libertad*, Roberto Thieme, in exile in Ecuador since 29 June, returned illegally to Chile and announced that he would launch actions. The government ordered his capture on 22 July, but before that he managed to meet with Navy captain Hugo Castro who informed him that a new strike must begin 25 July to paralyse the country and create the conditions for the coup. He asked *Patria y Libertad* to contribute to this by sabotaging railroads, roads, and oil pipelines but avoiding major damage. The Navy had to indicate the objectives and provided the explosives. One of the targets was the ENAP pipeline from San Fernando to San Vicente. The explosion in Curico caused 9 wounded and 2 dead. Another target was the high-voltage lines destroyed by *Patria y Libertad*; depriving the central region of electricity. The actions of the terrorist groups also led to the killing at home of Captain Arturo Araya, Captain of the Navy and Naval Aide to the President on 26 July. The Right then launched a press campaign accusing Cubans and the GAP of the death of the officer. The persons in charge were nevertheless found, and the authorities discovered that they were led by a former Navy cadet. According to Jorge Escalante, the shooter, posted on the balcony facing the house of Araya, was also linked to the navy[138].

On Thursday 9 August, President Allende restructured his cabinet once again, incorporating the three Commanders of the Armed Forces and the Director General of the Carabineros. The new cabinet of "national security", was defined by the President as a "last chance". On the same day, announced by this cabinet, the CUT convened a demonstration in Santiago. The president and the secretary-general of the organization were hard pressed to make their voices heard in the face of the dissatisfaction and disapproval shown by the workers about the attitude of the military and their entry into the government. Rolando Calderón's assertions, noting that a decisive phase was live and it was necessary to prepare the popular defence, contrasted with the disorder, the relative demoralisation and the state of demobilization that afternoon.

Personal intervention by General Prats helped thwart the *Tancazo*, but in turn made him one of the primary targets for plotters of the next attempt. (Wikimedia Commons)

At the end of August 1973, the political preparation of the coup became intense. The strike by the truckers continued for more than one month. The terrorist attacks were innumerable. *Patria y Libertad* announced that it was going underground to follow the "example" that soldiers had set on 29 June. On 22 August, the PDC voted the statement that "the government is not limited to isolated violations of the Constitution and the law, but has made it a permanent system of conduct", and asked the High Command of the military to "put an immediate end to all the aforementioned situations". This statement appeared as a legitimation for a possible coup d'etat. In fact, at a time when insurrectionary agitation and political and institutional conflict reached its peak, the coup was already prepared. On the walls of Santiago the graffiti "Jakarta arrives" was appearing; alluding to the military repression in Indonesia which, in the middle of the 1960s, caused nearly a million victims.[139]

Final Plot

As of 29 June the discussions were multiplying within the FF. AA. Some military sectors, while maintaining a certain political autonomy, were already considered as linked to the projects of the Right and converged in their common interest to isolate the elements loyal to the government. The draft coup d'etat began in the Navy, which had always been the most hostile to Allende since his election. On 12 July 1973, Admiral Merino received the Cochayuyo Anti-Insurgency Action Plan, which provided for the country to be divided into different sections and for each to draw up a plan of action against a possible insurgency. Foremost, he made the decision to directly oppose the government. Of all the military involved in the coup, Merino was the most ideological, his uncompromising Catholicism gave his fight against Marxism a crusading appearance. He was also the most determined, and the one who didn't fear a possible civil war even against one or more elements of the military. He decided that the Cochayuyo plan had to be the base for a new coup attempt and adapted it to the new circumstances. Merino knew that he could count on Admiral Carvajal, Chief of the Defence Staff. There remained the problem of the commander of the Navy, Admiral Montero, who was a moderate: however, Montero was isolated and he was often in Santiago at the request of Allende before participating in the government in August[140]. The conspirators had to dismiss General Prats, who maintained his loyalty to the president, while the garrison of Santiago and the command of the military institutes remained in the hands of those close generals Sepúlveda and Pickering.

Admiral Jose Toribio Merino was the most ideological opponent of Allende, and the primary planner of the coup of 11 September 1973. (Wikimedia Commons)

The national security cabinet suffered its first crisis just a week after its formation, with the resignation of the C-in-C FACh, Air General César Ruiz Danyau – who occupied the portfolio of Public Works and Transport, a crucial sector with the truckers' strike. The crisis began the previous week when Ruiz wanted to resign from the cabinet to protest against the Mayor of Santiago's action against the strike. Allende reacted with a demand for Ruiz to give up the command of the air force: the general initially resisted, but then accepted on 17 August 1973. He was replaced as minister by General Humberto Magliochetti, while General Gustavo Leigh Guzman was appointed the C-in-C FACh. This appointment was surprising because Leigh was considered an opponent of Allende.

The dismissal of Ruiz caused quite some trouble within the air force. On 20 August, 120 officers met at the air base in El Bosque to protest. Leigh then gave the order to move the fighter planes to Concepcion to prevent rebel officers from using them. Obedience to the constitutional government still prevented an armed confrontation with the government.[141]

Attack on General Prats

During the afternoon of 21 August 1973, General Prats was targeted during a demonstration of women in front of his private residence. The protesters included about 300 women and nine generals in civilian clothes, and resulted in a confrontation with the police. Immediately afterwards, and on the pretext of excusing the involvement of his wife, General Oscar Bonilla (reputed as the officer most directly associated with Frei) met Prats and publicly declared that the demonstration of the women was a result of the discontent in the High Command, and thus announced his resignation in order to avoid bloodshed within the military.

Shortly after, General Prats received a visit from President Allende and told him what happened. Allende reacted by summoning generals loyal to the government to his residence. Measures were taken to remedy the situation: demand for the retirement of the officers involved in the preparation of the coup d'etat, displacement and replacement of some of them, strengthening of the police garrison in the capital, preparation of a plan the defence of loyal troops in collaboration with the workers. That same night, CUT leaders and officers coordinated defence preparations. The loyalist generals (among them was Pinochet) informed the government that the adoption of the proposed measures would ensure the military defeat of the plotters if they took action.

On 22 August, Prats, who had no doubt that an uprising was in preparation against the government, but didn't know who was leading it, reunited the Generals who were in Santiago in order that they could pronounce on the incidents in front of his house by their wives. The majority of the Generals present refused to condemn the event, two or three approved it, and only four or five, including Pinochet, supported Prats. Amongst the supporters there were officers who commanded the troops in the capital but, on Thursday 23, overwhelmed by the impossibility of maintaining the High Command in a constitutional manner, General Carlos Prats resigned from his positions as Minister of the Defence and the C-in-C. At this moment, General Sepúlveda (chief of the garrison of Santiago), and Pickering (Director of the Military Institute) – the two commanders of the largest number of troops in the capital, and last obstacles to the coup – resigned. Prats was replaced in the government by General Rolando González, and at the post of C-in-C by Augusto Pinochet. Allende was convinced that

Pinochet was, after Prats, the officer most committed and faithful to the law and the Constitution[142].

On 21 August – the day of the stormy meeting of the FACh and the demonstration of women against Prats – the admirals met in Valparaíso to discuss the appointment of Admiral Arellano as Minister of Finance. They rejected the Navy's participation in the government. They also advised Montero that he was no longer a cohesive factor in the Navy. The latter presented his resignation to Allende on the 24th; who refused. The admirals insisted and Allende declared himself in conflict with the Navy. On 3 September, Allende finally accepted the resignation of Montero, and his replacement by Merino whose appointment was to be announced on the 7th.[143] But that day, the press had already been informed and Allende refused to announce the change. In the High Command, the elimination of the generals loyal to the government sanctioned the defeat of the constitutional positions. The military sectors were united and prepared.

Pinochet was summoned to Allende along with the Minister of Defence, Orlando Letelier; the Secretary General of the Government, Fernando Flores; the Secretary General of the PCCh, Luis Corvalán; the Director of Intelligence, the socialist Eduardo Paredes; and the General Orlando Urbina. The president and defence minister were briefed on Pinochet's plan for internal security, as the army chief of staff, on 16 July. Allende talked about the possibility of a confrontation between the government and the opposition, and pressure upon the military to remove it from its constitutional role. Urbina replied that a solution to the crisis had to be found through a referendum or an agreement with the opposition, otherwise violence would increase. At the end of the meeting, driving back with Urbina, Pinochet asked if he would be General Rojo – a Spanish officer who remained loyal to the Spanish Republican government in July 1936 – in case of a clash. Urbina answered no, just like Pinochet.[144]

At the end of August, preparations for the coup increased. Taking advantage of the law on the control of weapons, even exceeding its field of application, the High Command developed a systematic program of raids, harassment and persecution of workers and the Left, in factories and public places. In some cities and regions, it established real areas of occupation, regardless of legal grounds and the civil authorities. Leigh was particularly harsh in the application of this law, especially in the factories. At the Lanera Austral plant in Punta Arena, a military operation led to a shooting and the death of a worker. On the night of 7 September, a unit of the FACh overran Sumar textile factory and there was a shooting. According to the UP, it was the soldiers who mistreated the workers. After a conversation between Leigh and Letelier, the soldiers left the factory[145]. The incident raised fears among the military that the Left had developed military forces. The next day, Allende asked for the raids in the factories to stop, and asked the director of the police, Alfredo Joignant, to conduct an investigation into the events of Sumar. The conflict with the FACh began.

During the first week of September, Admiral Merino openly defied the government. He announced the discovery of a leftist infiltration on the *Almirante Latorre* and *Wadleigh* vessels organized by the Senator and Secretary General of PS, Altamirano; the MAPU Deputy Secretary, Óscar Guillermo Garretón; and the head of the MIR, Miguel Enríquez. In fact it was NCOs and sailors who made known to the leaders of the Left the preparations for the coup. Detected by the officers, they were arrested and mistreated. To support Merino, the commanders of six ships refused to sail to join Operation UNITAS on the pretext that they feared that their ships were also infiltrated. The Navy was close to chaos.[146]

On 8 September, Merino gathered the admirals and made the decision to begin the uprising. Carvajal announced that the FACh followed the Navy, but he was not certainty about Pinochet because the C-in-C appeared to be a loyalist soldier.[147] Pinochet's positioning was of crucial importance: if he joined the plot, the military would face Allende united and had the best chance of succeeding. If he remained loyal to the government, the military would be split and Chile would experience the civil war like Spain had in 1936.

Air General Leigh's appointment as the C-in-C FACh, and then his decision to side with coup plotters, were the first steps that enabled the military mutiny against Allende. (Wikimedia Commons)

The increasing pressure on military leaders to overthrow Allende grew rapidly in the last months of his presidency. Pinochet, considered not only loyal to Allende, but also an inefficient plotter, would be key to the success of the coup; a few days after assuming the role of C-in-C, Chilean military leaders targeted him and urged him to act. Highlighting divisions within the UP and between opposition leaders, they lamented that "the political party has become more important than the country," that the "respect for human life" is lost. "By their very nature, the armed forces were ideologically... antagonistic to Marxism", insisted the authors of this memorandum, and they signed in praying for Pinochet to decide the fate of Chile.[148]

On 8 September, General Arellano warned Pinochet that an uprising was in preparation: the latter didn't answer. The next day he was received, with Urbina, by Allende who announced his decision to organize a referendum to get out the political crisis. When Pinochet returned to his office, he received General Leigh and Admiral Huidobro, who handed him a message from Merino. The note indicated that the uprising would take place on the 11 September and asked for the support of Pinochet and Leigh. The commander of the FACh, and the C-in-Cs of the High Command and the Army gave their agreement. Admiral Huidobro returned to Valparaíso to inform Merino.[149]

If the commanders of the FF. AA were united in their putschist will, there remained one last force that could still defend Allende, the Carabineros. These had been put to the test in recent years. They were in charge of public order in a country where riots were frequent, and were accused of not following the orders of the government. The tension crystallized on 29 June, during the *Tancazo*, when the deputy director of the Carabineros, General Ramón Viveros ordered the La Moneda guard not to fire at the 2nd Armoured Regiment, thus contravening Allende's orders. Viveros was retired and replaced by Jorge Urrutia. The chiefs of the Carabineros were faithful to the government except for General Mendoza and General Arturo Yovane. The latter, stationed in Valparaíso, made contact with Merino,

Arellano and Carvajal before his transfer to Santiago in August 1973. It was a born conspirator who took care to visit all units to assess their degree of loyalty. He thus contacted many colonels and captains. He also chose the new leader of the Carabineros, General Mendoza; a popular man but without political depth. On the evening of 10 September, he was assured of the support of the Carabineros School, and its machine-gun section in particular.[150]

Military Plan of the Centre Group

The plan for the coup, baptised 'Military plan of the Centre Group', was prepared by General Arellano in the night of 10 September. Detailed in the Plan Ariete, it fixed the means and objectives of each unit as well as the phases of their actions. The first phase included the control of essential services, the second aimed to prevent violence or mass actions from the civilian population. So it was not a simple plan of attack, but of occupation of the city, trying to ensure the integrity of the infrastructure and to prevent not only armed resistance but also sabotage and the agitation. The plan of the military was as follows: in the south, San Bernardo Infantry School had to occupy the bridges on the Maipo River and then initiate a pincer movement by Vicuña Mackenna, encircling the Cordón industrial to reach the centre of Santiago. To the west, the Maipo, Valparaíso, Coraceros Cavalry and Viña del Mar Infantry Regiments had to seize Lo Prado Tunnel and advanced to encircle the Cordón industrial of the Central Station as well as La Villa Portales and UTE University. To the north-east, units of the Yungay and San Felipe Regiments had to protect base services and support the Buin Regiment to the north. To the north, 770 men from the Guardia Vieja Regiment of Los Andes had to block the Chacabuco road and launched an encirclement movement west to San Miguel. In the centre of Santiago, it was not only one unit that acted but four: the NCO School, the Armoured Regiment, two companies and 12 artillery pieces of the Tacna regiment, and part of the Infantry School. Overall, it was an overwhelming machine of 3,000 men encircling the city and marching on the centre. To the north-east, the Buin Regiment, the Military Academy Battalion, and the FACh were in reserves for the Centre group. Soldiers wore salmon-coloured scarves so they could recognize each other and received 3 days of food.

If the Navy was to occupy Valparaíso, the first port and second city of the country, the FACh was also entrusted with a key role in the coup. On 10 September, during a meeting with Pinochet, General Leigh proposed bombing La Moneda in case of resistance from Allende, adding that the attack would be accurate and the pilots were ready. It was also agreed that an airplane would be available for the president and his family to escape. Leigh summoned his closest generals and informed them of the action of the 11th. Preparations began. He excluded two generals: Alberto Bachelet who sympathized with the government and Carlos Dinator.[151] At the Los Cerillos air base, the FACh leader received 20 pilots and co-pilots who were to pilot the DC-3 for troop transport and equipment for the putsch. The previous weekend he sent his best fighter airplanes, the Hawker Hunter, to Concepcion under the protection of the Navy, knowing that these planes could reach Santiago in just 25 minutes. They were at the heart of the Trueno Plan which defined FACh's participation in the coup.

On 10th September, Allende had a bad day. At noon, a meeting of the government showed the disastrous situation for the country. Conflict with the Navy, and the opposition, increased after a provocative speech by Altamirano; the Enap pipeline was sabotaged aggravating the lack of fuel, and the country had wheat for only four days after a strike in the port of San Antonio. Allende decided to announce political measures including a referendum. This decision was a political bomb since the political committee of the UP rejected proposals for an agreement with the PDC; Allende only received support from the PCCh. He decided to announce the referendum the following day during a visit in UTE University[152].

Allende clearly feared the worst, but he seemed calm. Nine days before the coup, he told his family that he was ready to die if necessary. A Chilean historian spoke about the story of the leftist reformist president, José Manuel Balmaceda, who committed suicide in 1891 after the failure of his progressive reforms[153]. The president still thought that a coup d'etat would involve only one of the three branches, and not all of the armed forces; this would be treachery for him, especially since he had always taken care to keep in contact with the commanders, and satisfied many requests from the military. He imagined that during a coup, the regime's defence would be carried out by soldiers fighting against rebel units. The population should not intervene but just support. The *Tancazo* reinforced Allende in his certainties. He perceived a serious situation only in the Navy and he thought that by keeping Montero, he would hinder the aspirations of the sailors. He nevertheless considered the possibility of applying the anti-insurgency plan; the Hercules Plan prepared by Pinochet to neutralize the ultras groups[154], but excluded all ideas of popular resistance because he knew that the UP parties had no real military capability, and he didn't try to encourage it because he loathed the idea of civil war[155].

On the afternoon of 10 September, Leigh ordered the Air Group 7 commander to prepare for a mission on Santiago, with 12 of his 18 Hawkers armed with rockets. This team was reinforced by four planes from group 9 of Puerto Montt. The QG of the coup was installed at the command of telecommunications of the army in Penalolén. It was the only place in Santiago where it was possible to communicate with all units of the FF. AA. On the evening of 10 September, the staff distributed orders for the action to all the divisions through personal notes. Major Siebert brought them to Concepcion for General Carrasco, the leader of the powerful 3rd Division[156].

International involvement

As Tanya Harmer wrote, '...Chile became a theatre of the struggle between revolution and reaction on the continent from mid-1973 onwards...'[157] Many protagonists were involved in this fight, including the USA and Cuba, but also several other countries and leftist movements in Latin America and elsewhere.

The involvement of the United States in the preparation of the coup remains poorly known, despite the publication of many declassified documents. As John Dinges concluded, although released documents did offer a lot of information, they were still incomplete.[158] However, the latest official report on the role of the CIA – known as '2000 Hinchey Report' – summarized:

'Although CIA did not instigate the coup that ended Allende's government on 11 September 1973, it was aware of coup-plotting by the military, had ongoing intelligence collection relationships with some plotters, and—because CIA did not discourage the takeover and had sought to instigate a coup in 1970—probably appeared to condone it.'[159]

After the parliamentary elections in March 1973, preparations for an impending confrontation between Left and Right became more urgent. The Nixon administration clearly sympathized with the plot, but feared the failure of what was, meanwhile, three-years of efforts to bring down the Chilean government, and was thus frustrated with the slow progress of related preparations – even more so once the *Tancazo* failed to bring down Allende. US leaders were aware that the High Command of the military was divided and that constitutionalists were still strong. Thus, Washington developed a preference for maintaining

As of September 1973, the FACh had received a total of 39 Hunters, of which 33 were still available and 31 operational. All wore the standard camouflage pattern (applied prior to delivery), consisting of dark sea grey (BS381C/638, FS 361734) and dark green (BS381C/241, FS 34079) on upper surfaces and sides, while bottom surfaces were left in a high speed silver finish. Two or three Hunter F.Mk 71s from the first batch had the insignia of the Grupo 7 applied on the front fuselage. Between them was J-705 depicted here: this aircraft was lost in an accident on 12 June 1972, when its pilot, Captain Meirelles ejected safely. (Artwork by Tom Cooper)

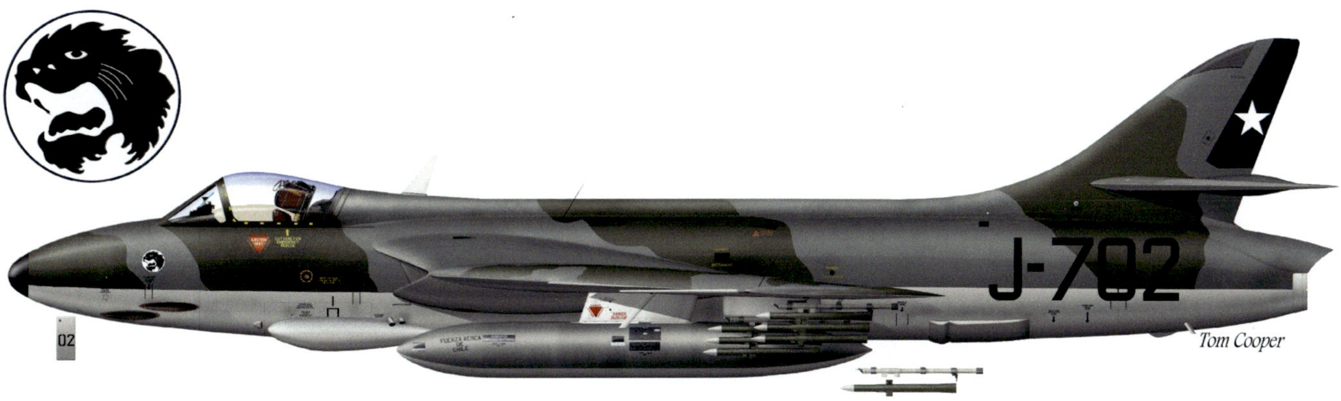

This is a reconstruction of the Hunter F.Mk 71 with serial number J-702, flown by Colonel Mario 'Libra' Lopez Tobar during attack on transmitter of Radio Corporacion in La Florida, near Vicuña Mackenna, early on the morning of 11 September 1973. It was one of 12 fighter-bombers known to have been deployed in support of the coup: the others known to have been included wore serials J-702, J-704, J-709, J-711, J-712 (all from Grupo 9), J-722, J-726 (from Grupo 7), and J-731 (Grupo 9). Armament confirmed as deployed on that day – so also for attacks on Moneda Palace – included Hispano R80 Sura unguided rockets, and 30mm ADEN cannons installed internally. Inset is showning the insignia of the Grupo 9; as of September 1973, this was usually applied only on the front fuselage (subsequently, it was frequently applied below the top of the fin, too). (Artwork by Tom Cooper)

The FACh had a total of six Hunter FR.Mk 71s as of September 1973. They were camouflaged and marked in same fashion as F.Mk 71 fighter-bombers, and had their serials applied in the same fashion – including the prefix 'J-' – on both sides of the rear fuselage, the top side of the left, and the lower side of the right wing. As far as is known, none of them carried any unit insignias as of 1973. Like in the case of all of Hunters delivered to Chile, their primary armament consisted of Hispano R80 Sura rockets installed in 'banks' of three on Mk.12 launch rails, details of which are illustrated on insets below the main illustration. Up to four such rails could be carried under each wing (one of these on the outboard underwing pylon). Other weapons known to be in use, as of 1973, included bombs made by Spanish company EXPAL, based on US-designs of Mk.81 and Mk.82. (Artwork by Tom Cooper)

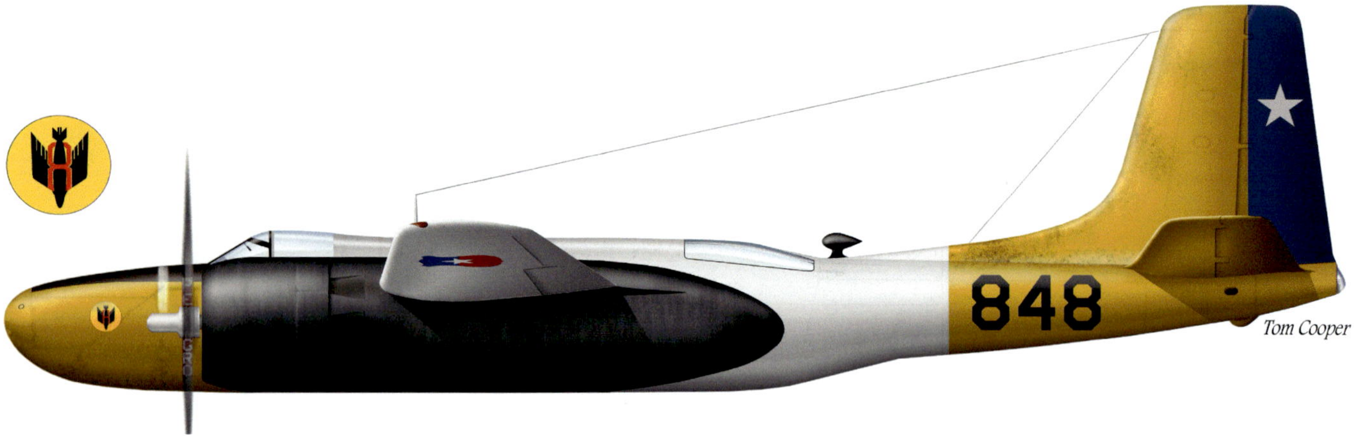

Nominally, the Grupo 8 of the FACH still had 10 B-26Cs, TB-26Bs and TB-26Ds on strength as of September 1973. The latter two variants served as conversion trainers and some of them wore gaudy markings, like this TB-26D: the nose, rear fuselage, fin and horizontal stabilisers were all painted in yellow, the centre fuselage and the wing were left in natural metal overall, while engine nacelles were painted in black. Notable is the application of the unit insignia on the nose, and a big serial on the rear fuselage; national markings were applied on the top surface of the right, and bottom surface of the left wing only. (Artwork by Tom Cooper)

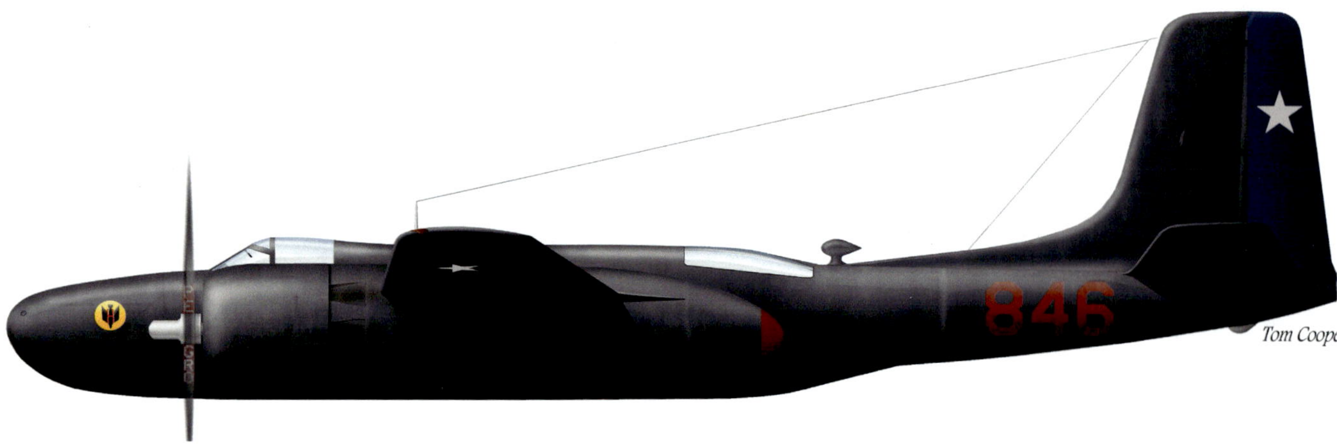

When the FACH's fleet of B-26s was re-defined as that of the COIN, in 1970, most of remaining B-26Ds were overpainted in black overall, and armed with six machine guns in the nose. Serials were applied in red on the rear fuselage, while remaining markings were limited to white stars on the fin, top surface of the right, and bottom surface of the left wing, and the usual unit insignia on the nose. The fleet was badly worn out by the early 1970s, and flew very little. Nevertheless, Chilean Invaders flew several 'intimidation' flights during the coup of 11 September 1973: one of was involved in the search for surviving GAPs in Santiago, too. (Artwork by Tom Cooper)

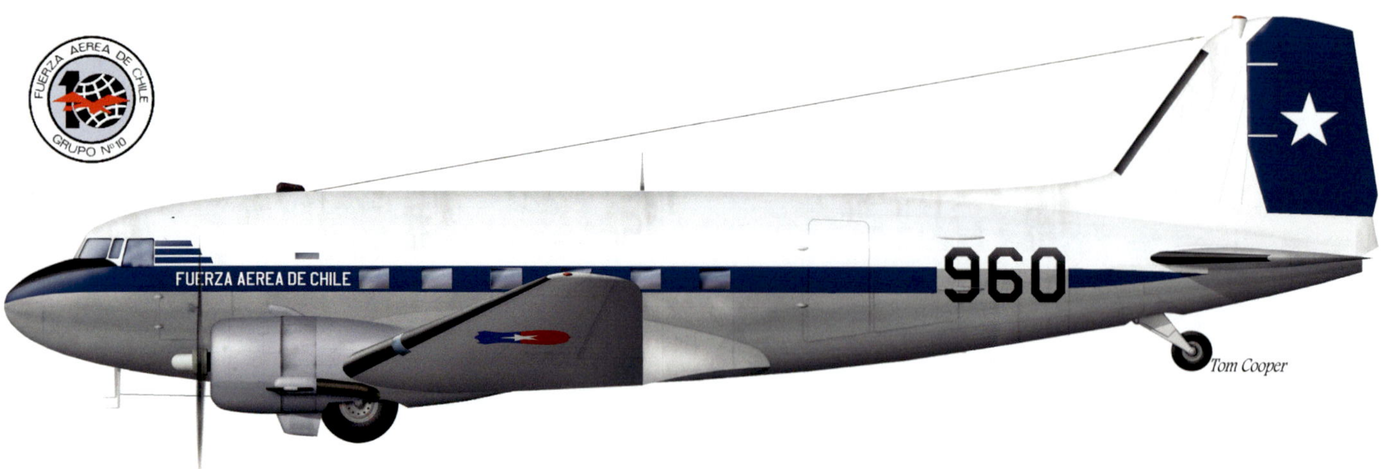

C-47s of the FACH were operated by Grupo 10 and generally wore civilian-style livery as of September 1973. This included white on the top surfaces of the fuselage and the fin, a blue cheat-line, and aluminium on the lower fuselage, wings, engine nacelles, and horizontal stabilisers. Except for large serials on the rear fuselage, top surface of the left- and bottom surface of the right wing, and the usual set of national insignia, they received sizeable service titles between the cockpit and the first cabin window. In addition to C-47s, the Grupo 10 operated several C-54s. (Artwork by Tom Cooper)

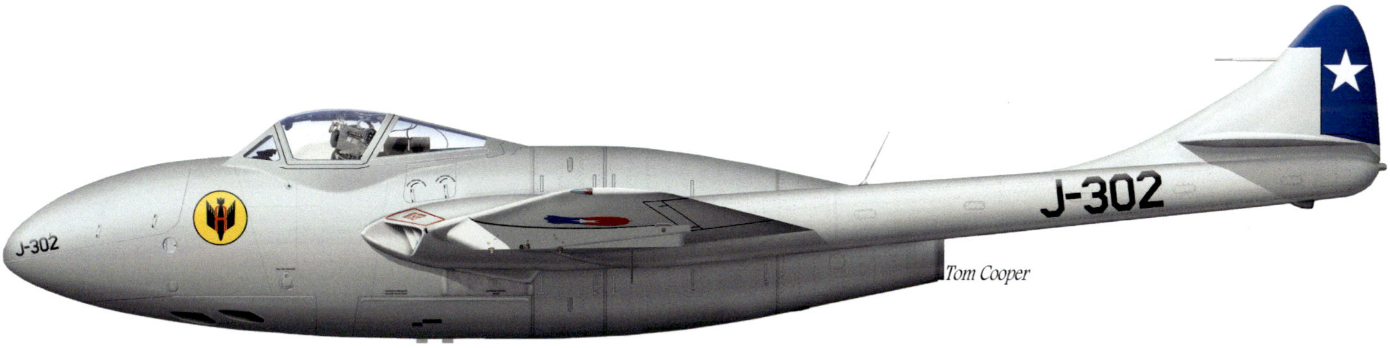

For most of the 1960s, and in early 1970s, the FACH's fleet of T.Mk 55s used to wear high-speed silver finish overall. As usually on all of Chilean military aircraft, large serials were applied in black on the top surface of the left- and the bottom surface of the right wing; while full national markings were applied on the top surface of the right- and the bottom surface of the left wing. Additional serials were applied on the boom and repeated – in much smaller format – on the nose. Like Invaders of that unit, all the Vampires also wore the insignia of Grupo 8 on their forward fuselage. This example is shown equipped with an underwing hardpoint, which enabled the carriage of bombs up to the calibre 500lbs (250 Kilogram). (Artwork by Tom Cooper)

As of September 1973, Grupo 8 of the FACh had one Vampire T.Mk 55, four Vampire T.Mk 11s and six Sea Vampire T.Mk 22s in service. All were based at Cerro Moreno and served as advanced trainers with ground attack as their secondary purpose (for which they could be armed with Mk 12 launch rails for Hispano R80 Sura unguided rockets). The sole T.Mk 55 still in service was the former J-302, meanwhile re-serialled as J-304, and wearing this unique camouflage in dark sea grey and dark green on top surfaces and sides, and sky S on bottom surfaces. (Artwork by Tom Cooper)

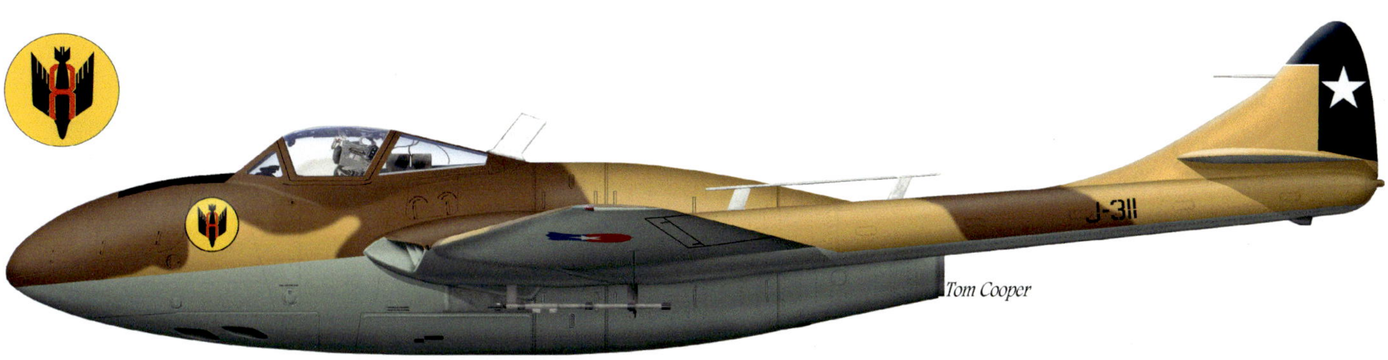

While put on alert for action on 11 September 1973, Vampires of Grupo 8 seem not to have been deployed during the coup. By the time, all of T.Mk 11s and T.Mk 22s have received the same, 'desert' camouflage pattern consisting of sand or light stone, and dark earth (BS381C/350) or brown (ICI F407-1815) on top surfaces and sides. Undersides were painted in sky S (or Sky Blue, BS381C/101). All were equipped with Mk. 12 launch rails for Sura unguided rockets: these were attached to the lower wing surfaces with help of simple metal strips in 'V' form. (Artwork by Tom Cooper)

The FACh received a total of 18 F-80Cs (built between 1947 and 1949) starting in October 1956. Originally, all were left in natural metal overall, and wore large black serials on the rear fuselage in range J-330 to J-347. The fleet originally served as advanced trainers and fighter-bombers alongside Vampires with Grupo 7 at Los Cerillos AB. Fifteen remained in service by 1967. (Artwork by Tom Cooper)

In 1967, seven surviving F-80Cs were equipped with Mk. 12 launch rails for unguided rockets, and re-assigned to Grupo 9, based at La Chamiza AB, outside Puerto Montt, in southern central Chile. At the same opportunity, all were camouflaged in disruptive camouflage pattern consisting of light grey, dark brown and dark green on top surfaces and sides (this differed from aircraft to aircraft), and light sky S on undersurfaces. They retained their big black serials, but these were applied in a slightly different font. Later in the 1970s, they were re-assigned to Magellanes-based Grupo 12 and received corresponding unit insignia – resulting in the look illustrated here. (Artwork by Tom Cooper)

The first four T-33As armed trainers arrived in Chile in October 1956. They received serials J-314 to J-317 and were assigned to Grupo 7 at Los Cerillos. The second batch of nine (serials J-318 to J-326) followed in 1959, when the entire fleet was transferred to Grupo 9. A pair of RT-33As – serials J-327 and J-328 – equipped for reconnaissance was acquired around the same time. In late 1960s, the fleet was reconfigured to the RT-33A standard, and partially equipped with Mk. 12 launch rails for unguided rockets. As of September 1973, Chilean T-33As have served with La Chamiza/Puerto Montt-based Grupo 9. (Artwork by Tom Cooper)

Chile received a total of 12 UH-1Ds and 22 UH-1Hs by 1973. All were left in their original livery, consisting of olive drab overall. Several had the roof of their cockpit and the cabin painted in white, and all seem to have had a wide band around the boom painted in orange. Their serials ranged from H-75 to H-96 and were always applied on the side doors, as was the title Fuerza Aerea de Chile. Several UH-1s are known to have been flown by crews involved in the coup on 11 September 1973, but no details about their identities are available. This example, former 67-18561 (10064) of the US Army is known to have been delivered to Chile in 1967. (Artwork by Tom Cooper)

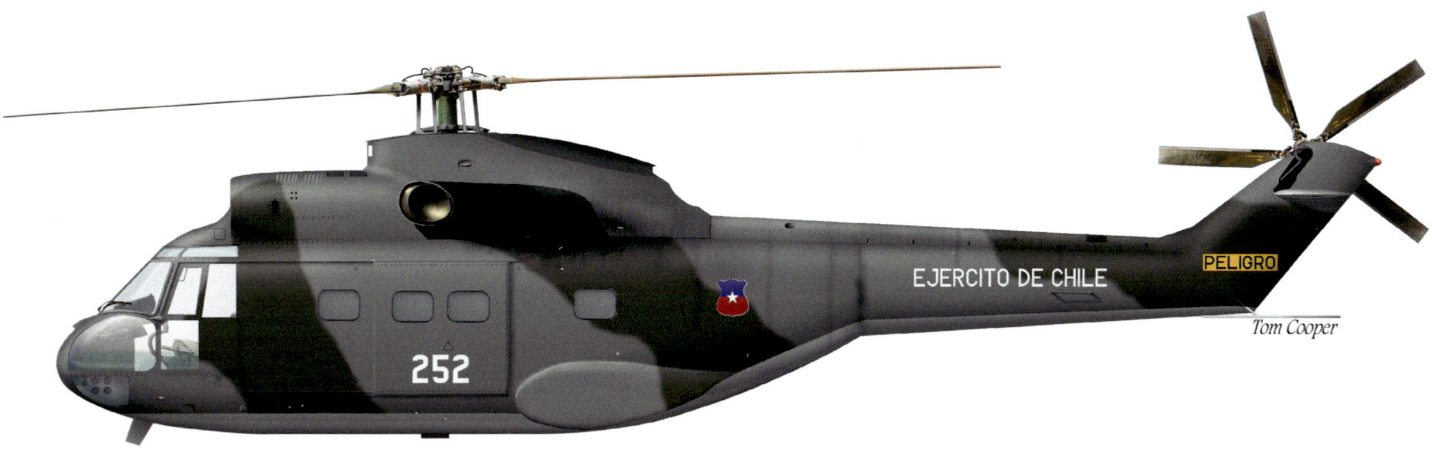

Ejercito de Chile – Chilean Army – obtained three SA.330H Puma helicopters) in the early 1970s. This was a 'hot and high' variant, with a more powerful Turbomeca-Turmo-IVC engine and the main rotor blades made of composites. At least one of these (serial unknown) was involved in the coup of 11 September 1973. The helicopter in question is known to have suffered combat damage from ground fire in form of 18 bullet holes. As of the time, Chilean Pumas were painted in dark sea grey and dark green on top surfaces and sides, and light grey on undersurfaces. Large serials and service-title were applied in white. Notable is that the national insignia had a thin white outline, as often on Chilean Army's vehicles. (Artwork by Tom Cooper

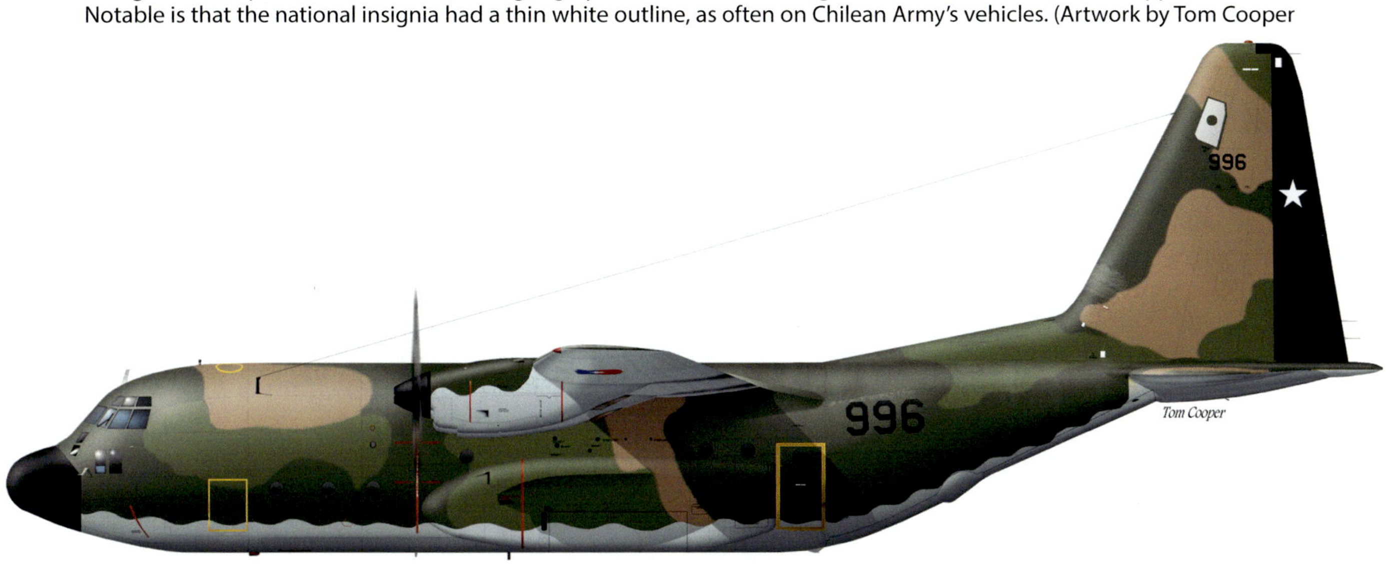

Two of little-known 'participants' of the coup against President Allende of 11 September 1973, were Lockheed C-130H Hercules transports: assigned to the Grupo 10, the aircraft in question – serials 995 and 996 – were deployed (together with at least one Boeing 707 and one Boeing 727) to transport troops between different parts of the country. As of September 1973, they wore the well-known 'South-East Asia' camouflage pattern of tan (FS 30219), green (FS34102) and dark green (FS 34079) on upper surfaces and sides, and light blue/grey on undersurfaces. (Artwork by Tom Cooper)

In August 1942, Chile received its first modern armour in the form of 12 M3A1 Stuart tanks provided by the USA within the Lend-Lease program. The original dozen were subsequently supplemented by another batch of 18, and then another of 23. They served with two motorised cavalry regiments and the School of Motorised Units. While most of these vehicles, with steel armour of 19mm – 51mm thickness, were withdrawn from service by 1969, at least a company remained operational long enough to see combat-like deployments during the *Tancazo* affair and then the coup of 11 September 1973. As far as is known, all were painted in olive drab as of 1973: some – but by far not all – received turret numbers applied in white. Notable is the application of the 'crossed sabres & tank' insignia, the generic symbol for the US Army's armour troops, in yellow, below the national insignia, which was usually outlined in white. (Artwork by David Bocquelet)

Between 1950 and 1970, Chile received US military aid worth US$91.4 million and excess stocks of military equipment worth $8 million. The latter included a total of 60 M24 Chaffee light tanks, delivered in the 1960s. Originally planned to replace old M3A1s, and although possessing good firepower relative to their weight and low silhouette, Chaffees proved ill-suited to the rather rugged topography of northern and central Chile. Later during their service they were re-deployed to southern Chile, where they proved far better suited to the local terrain. The type made next to no appearance during the coup of 1973, which is why very little is known about the looks of Chilean M24s during this period. As far as is known, they were all painted in olive drab overall, and had the national insignia applied on the turret side. (Artwork by David Bocquelet)

In 1954, Chile acquired a total of 17 M4A1E9 Sherman tanks, equipped with the 75mm M3 L/40 cannon. All had additional plates welded to the frontal armour on the turret and the hull. While the heaviest tank in arsenal of the Chilean military as of September 1973, they are not known to have seen any kind of action during the coup. As far as is known, all were painted in olive drab overall, and had received national markings and registration numbers applied in black. (Artwork by David Bocquelet)

The first 10 M41 Walker Bulldog light tanks arrived in Chile in 1964. Armed with the 76mm M32 cannon, these were light, but very fast tanks, with a high top speed. Following successful operational integration, the Chileans acquired 40 additional M41s in 1970, and they formed the backbone of the two armoured regiments as of 1973. While the USA initially supported Chilean operations of this type by providing training, spares and ammunition free of charge, the Chileans were quick in establishing support infrastructure at home – which in turn enabled the military to retain its M41s even after facing severe embargoes in the wake of the coup of 1973. As usual, Chilean M41s were pained in olive drab overall, and wore the standard set of national markings and those of the armoured corps. Several of the M41s involved in the *Tancazo* affair, and the coup of 11 September 1973, were seen wearing large turret numbers, as shown here. (Artwork by David Bocquelet)

Another type that played a prominent role during the *Tancazo* affair in June 1973 was the M113A armoured personnel carrier; a column of which was led by Colonel Federico Souper in person. Chile received an unknown number of M113s in 1970 and 1971, free of charge, before Washington stopped providing help. All were painted in olive drab overall. While M113s involved in the *Tancazo* went into action still wearing their full insignia – including individual hull numbers – those involved in the coup of 11 September 1973, usually had all of their insignia crudely overpainted. (Artwork by David Bocquelet)

At least ten M5 half-tracks were delivered by the USA to Chile within the Military Assistance Program during World War II. Additional M3A1 armoured personnel carriers – some with, and some without the ring for the heavy machine gun – followed during the 1950s. Painted in olive drab overall, all wore the usual set of national markings and the Armoured Corps insignia on hull sides and the rear. Registration numbers were usually applied on the side of the forward fuselage. Reinforced through additional acquisitions (primarily from Israel) in the 1970s, the type remained in service as weapons carrier and recovery vehicle well into the 1990s. (Artwork by David Bocquelet)

Map of FACH's air bases as of September 1973. (Map by Tom Cooper)

A map of major roads and crucial public buildings and military installations in Santiago during the coup of 11 September 1973. (Map by Tom Cooper)

Retired Lieutenant-General Vernon Walters (2nd from left), at a meeting of the Military Intelligence Board in Washington, 1973. (CIA Photo)

Three leaders of the coup of 11 September 1973, from left to right: Leigh, Pinochet, and Merino. (Albert Grandolini Collection)

economic pressure upon Allende instead. When the World Bank was considering a loan to help Chile in July 1973, the State Department launched a successful diplomatic campaign that prompted the World Bank to postpone its decision. Furthermore, when officials of the CIA and State Department discussed clandestine operations in early June 1973, Nixon's new deputy secretary of state for Latin American affairs, Jack Kubisch, concluded that, 'a military coup seemed to be a non-starter' – and a representative of the CIA agreed. Those present also agreed that the growing national criticism of the government's secret operations increased the risks of greater involvement. When Prats resigned on 23 August, the Nixon administration judged his successor, Pinochet as a man without a stature and unable to conduct a coup.[160]

Nevertheless, the presence of Vernon Walters, Deputy Director for the US Central Intelligence Agency, in Chile is often declared for a 'confirmation' of the US involvement in the coup – a thesis supported by some declassified files. Walters was well-known for his contacts with the Brazilian military, and provided help to coup plotters that overthrew President Goulart in 1964. Nevertheless, it is obvious that the conspiracy was not exclusively inspired by the USA or led by Washington. On the contrary, other international actors – foremost Brazil – had stepped up their aid to the coup plotters. Indeed, the Brazilians strongly encouraged and supported the military plotters and their civilian supporters, prompting ever more top officers to lean in favour of the regime in Brasilia. Indeed, the Brazilian ambassador to Santiago proposed, '...cooperative planning, inter-embassy coordination, and joint efforts...' to the US ambassador Davis, which left the latter to conclude that, '...the Brazilians supported and trained the conspirators'. Indeed, the documentation released in 2009 has indicated that the Brazilian support was 'decisive for the success of the coup in Chile'.[161]

Bolivia had been effectively used by the Right to channel weapons into Chile. In mid-1973, *Patria y Libertad* leader Roberto Thieme is known to have travelled to the country, Paraguay, and Argentina in search of support. The involvement of the neighbouring dictatorships was useful for Washington, especially when Nixon's administration was shattered by the Watergate Affair.

Last-Minute Moves

On Monday 10 September, the US ambassador, having been informed that the coup would take place the next day, stood carefully ready to help. Returning to Santiago the day before, Davis told Washington that he had informed the Chilean Navy that the embassy was 'flexible and ready to meet any requirement'. He added: 'At this moment, our best posture is to continue to do business, and the US initiative would be difficult to explain and probably misinterpreted'.[162]

On their side, the Cubans were concerned for Allende. Havana had long been waiting for an armed confrontation in Chile. Similarly, after the *Tancazo*, the Soviet Foreign Ministry warned that an 'open armed battle' was a serious possibility, but that the UP did not have a common policy towards the Chilean armed forces.[163]

In this context, in late July, Manuel Piñeiro and Carlos Rafael Rodriguez arrived in Chile to deliver a letter from Castro to Allende. The letter referred to the need for Allende to prepare for the confrontation. The *lider maximo* implored the Chilean president to face a direct struggle as a leader of mass resistance. 'Do not forget for a moment the tremendous strength of the Chilean working class', insisted Castro. He suggested that workers could 'paralyse' a coup, prevent hesitations and, if his actions were precise, decide the fate of Chile. He argued that "the enemy should know that the Chilean working class is warned and ready to go into action." Castro also reminded Allende that his leadership was "before all the key to the situation," and he ended by asking how Havana could help.[164]

It was at this time that Allende asked the Cubans to prepare defence plans for the presidential palace. Allende had been clear that in the event of a military attack, he would go to La Moneda. Cuba's immediate concern was the strategic vulnerability of this place; for the Cubans, La Moneda was a vulnerable low-level building surrounded by larger ones. 'From a military point of view, it was a disaster!'[165], recalled Oña. If Havana had been in charge of the strategic decisions, he would have sent Allende to carry out a prolonged resistance in the periphery of the city, where the workers began to organize to resist an attack.

The Cubans could not change Allende's determination to confront the military intervention from the presidential palace, and Castro maintained an uncompromising line, although his instincts were opposed: nothing without Allende's authorization. However, when Allende showed Cuban plans to Prats and to General Sepúlveda, it clearly weakened his defence and risked a leak to the conspirators if Pinochet saw the plans of exactly what the Cubans proposed. Perhaps the knowledge of the Cuban plan explained the brutality and the force used by the military plotters on 11 September to crush a left-wing unarmed and ill-prepared for an armed clash.

CHAPTER 5
COUP OF 11 SEPTEMBER 1973

To fully understand the different plans through which the coup was executed on 11 September, it should be noted that these would be expanded from a general order to a specific one. In other words, the Internal Defence Plan of the Armed Forces would be explained first, to later go on to detail the information obtained about the plans that were elaborated in the most important garrisons of the country, such as, Valparaíso, Santiago, Concepción and Punta Arenas. Behind the joint action of the FF. AA and Carabineros on 11 September, there was three-dimensional general planning. The latter was ultimately the explanatory factor as to why the military acted monolithically throughout the country. Next to it, each military garrison applied the zonal plans for internal security.

Seizure of Valparaíso

In relation to the military operation that was used in the First Naval Zone, with its seat in Valparaíso, the Navy devised an institutional plan for all its naval areas: this was called the Cochayuyo Plan[166]. Like most of the internal security plans that were used on 11 September, the Cochayuyo Plan was devised and had two well-defined parts. One was the maritime operation, which corresponded to that carried out by the National Squadron, and a second, which was the ground operation, where the activities developed by the marines were fundamental.

The maritime operations contained in the Cochayuyo Plan had two phases; a diversion, which was directed by the commander Cristian Storaker, and an offensive that was executed by the commander Mauricio Poisson. The first of them began on Monday 10th at 06:00 AM, and took the National Squad to Caldera where, supposedly they would participate in an exercise as part of Operation UNITAS. This type of joint operation with the US Marines was an activity that the Navy took place annually; the departure of the squadron would be interpreted as a routine activity that indicated to the authorities that the Navy was concerned with professional matters, and not about preparing a coup. Although the naval officers didn't recognize that there was prior coordination with the US Marines to carry out this "diversionary operation", other sources indicate that such contact did exist, and that when the coup was unleashed, the North American squadron was on the high seas attentive to what happened on the continent[167].

The offensive phase started at 05:30 AM on 11th September with the return of the National Squadron vessels to their respective objectives in the First Naval Zone. This second part of the maritime operation, contained in the Cochayuyo Plan, was confirmed at 05:40 AM, after which the crew learned the decision to depose the government. The beginning of the offensive plan for the maritime forces was scheduled for 08:30 AM and was executed as follows. At 05:00 AM, the ships that went to join the American fleet at Coquimbo changed course and returned to the central area. In less than an hour they took up their fighting position. In front of Quintero, the destroyers *Blanco*, *Encalada* and *Orella* were to protect the base of the FACh, in the port of Valparaíso the cruiser *Capitan Prat* (CL-03) and the destroyer *Aldea* (withdrawn from service in 1957, but reactivated for this occasion), pointed their cannons on the university Federico Santa Maria and Argentina Avenue; gathering places for inhabitants of the popular districts of the hills. Further south, the submarine *Simpson* protected the electrical station that powered the city. The destroyer *Cochrane* (former *USS Rooks*, DD-804 of the Fletcher-class) was in the port of San Antonio[168].

The operation carried out by the Navy on the ground, in the First Naval Zone, was executed by Rear Admiral Sergio Huidobro, who remembered having quartered his troops at 02:00 AM to start the

Cruiser *Captian Prat* (CL-03; former *USS Nashville*, CL-43) blocked the port of Valparaíso at the start of the coup on 11 September 1973. (Armada de Chile)

operation terrestrial proper at 05:00 AM. In the rest of the country, the Army, the Carabineros and the FACh had to come into action at 8:30 AM. The purpose of this shift was to deceive their opponents as to the place where the coup would take place. Among the tasks that were developed in the Valparaíso operation, it is possible to identify the occupation of the Customs Administration, the Prat and Barón docks and the two railway stations. The naval infantry came by truck from Viña del Mar and began to occupy the key places of the workers' rallies. Valparaíso was quickly under the control of the military.

At 04:30 AM on the morning of 11 September, Colonel Julio Polloni, at the Ministry of Defence, began to establish contact with the military and civilians involved in the execution of the Silence Plan in Santiago. In the planning developed by the plotters, specific tasks that facilitated the execution of the Internal Defence Plan were released. In this regard General Francisco Herrera recalled that "when the time came they felt the need to have an annexed telecommunications plan to keep the Armed Forces connected."[169] For this, the plotters had a specialized office called "Communications of the Armed Forces" (COFF.AA.), which was responsible for coordinating the Plan of Communications that has been devised, whose basic objective was to prevent sabotage to the communications of the operating forces. However, the true intentions of this operation were to silence the official radio stations that could eventually have hindered, with calls to subversion, the overthrow of the government that would be carried out by the Armed Forces and Carabineros. Only radio stations committed to the military operation, such as the radio stations Agricultura and Balmaceda, would remain.

Navy commandos began to act throughout the country. Those in Talcahueno were investing the ENAP plant in Concepcion, where the San Vicente Port Industrial Communication Center was located, and putting it out of service. A truck-full of sailors sent from Valparaíso attacked the UTE radio station in Santiago. In Valparaíso, the Navy neutralized 13 radio stations and 3 television channels. They also cut telephone lines in the city, with the exception of the Albatros system that was used by the Navy High Command and the phones that maintained links with regional commanders[170].

The Silence Plan didn't work in Santiago with the same efficiency as in Valparaíso. In the centre of the city, phone lines were broken but many continued to work. The plan didn't take into account that the palace of La Moneda had direct lines with several radio stations. The telephone lines to the residence of Tomás Moro, ministers, and the political leaders of the UP were also not cut. The main pro-government radio stations would not be neutralized by the army, but by the Navy or the bombing by the FACh. The plan even overlooked the existence of Radio Candelaria and Radio Magallanes. The latter would be followed all morning by 12 local radio stations. In a matter of hours, a speech recorded on a rudimentary magneto phone directly in the office of the President would become one of the most famous speeches in the history of Chile[171].

The heart of the plot's action was the city of Santiago for which the Plan A-1 was established. It assumed that the main actions would take place in the centre of the city. Once this area under control, the troops would be deployed in two rings. If the inner ring was subject to pressure from an opponent, there was an outer ring with the units located on the periphery. Taken between two forces, the pockets of resistance could be reduced in five days[172]. The army thus overestimated the firepower of the Left and particularly feared the Cordónes industriales.

The execution of Plan A-1 was coordinated by General Herman Brady. The command posts were handed over to General César Raúl Benavides, who operated with his troops from Vicuña Mackenna, to the east, and General Sergio Arellano, who was responsible for the mobilization of forces in the centre and the western area. The Palacio de la Moneda and the Civic District were entrusted to General Javier Palacios. The southern sector, from Avenida Departamental to San Bernardo, was entrusted to the general of the FACh, Mario Viveros. Towards the south, the troops of the Infantry School operated, and finally, in the north zone to the Mapocho River, the troops of the Maipo Regiment, led by Colonel Felipe Geiger, operated. Because of their mobility, the Carabineros, would deal with any other pockets of resistance that appeared, as well as taking responsibility for the area around La Moneda. Finally, the leaders of the different forces that acted in the military operation in Santiago did so from different locations. General Pinochet did it from the School of Telecommunications of Peñalolén, General Gustavo Leigh from the War Academy of the FACh, Admiral Patricio Carvajal from the dependencies of the General Staff, and General César Mendoza from the building of the General Directorate of Carabineros.[173]

The coup in the regions

By 0900 hrs, the High Command of the Chilean Armed Forces was in control of almost the entire country. All the strategic installations in Valparaíso were under the control of the Army and Navy. In Arica, in northern Chile, Colonel Mena arrested the governor and the mayor, and closed the border to Peru. At Iquique, General Carlos summoned the intendant to his own arrest. General Lagos took control of Antofagasta without resistance. The only incident happened in Police Station No. 4, where a young Carabinero who was a sympathiser of the PS, shot two officers that attempted to take control of the base. In Chuquicamata, Major Fernando Reveco deployed the Calama Regiment to take control of the World's largest copper mine, which was considered an outright 'nightmare' by the military. The area was expected to be under the control of leftist miners that could repel this attack and then construct an airstrip for Cuban aircraft, permitting deployment of reinforcements. However, the military encountered no resistance, while the manager of the mine – communist David Silberman – was arrested by the Calama Regiment. The other two potential trouble spots in the north, the industrial complex Soquimich in Tocopilla, and the UTE School in mines of Capiapo, were easily secured too.[174]

The coup of 11 September 1973 was a big operation, involving simultaneous movement of multiple units of the Army, Navy, and Air Force. The Army, especially, established a significant presence on all the major streets of all the towns and cities. This photograph shows a row of 5 M3 Stuarts (centre) and a White M3 scout car (left). (Albert Grandolini)

The military deployed in the Concepcion area followed the so-called Tijera Plan. Troops commanded by General Washington Carrasco quickly seized all strategic positions – including the local university – expending only a few bullets in the process. In order to avoid provoking local miners, Carrasco then decided not to deploy troops to Lota: instead, he left the Carabineros to secure this town.[175] Similarly, the Navy quickly established itself in control of Talcahuano.

In the centre of the country, Lieutenant-Colonel Ariosto Lapostol ordered the troops of the Arica Regiment on to the streets of La Serena and to arrest the communist intendant; in San Antonio, Colonel Contreras arrested all the leaders of the UP, while the troops of the Membrillar and Colchagua Regiments quickly established themselves in control over Rancagua and San Fernando. Two GAP operatives that were travelling to Santiago were arrested.

In Talca, troops under the control of Lieutenant-Colonel Jana secured the city, but left the socialist leader Germán Castro to flee to the mountains in the direction of Argentina. He was later arrested after a brief skirmish.[176]

In southern Chile, General Manuel Torrez de la Cruz deployed the troops of the 5th Division along the Australis Plan.[177] Temuco was secured by the Tucapel Regiment, while Valdivia was occupied by soldiers of the Cazadores and Maturana Regiments. The post of the Nelturne Carabineros in the Panguipulli Forest complex was surrounded by workers for most of the day, but their assault attempt the next morning, failed.[178] In Puerto Montt, General Hernan Leight established himself in control of the city, while in Punta Arenas the military acted on its own, without involvement of the Carabineros. Correspondingly, General Torres de la Cruz deployed tanks and

An M113 APC (foreground, left) and a M41 Walker Bulldog tank in the suburbs of Santiago, early in the morning of 11 September 1973. (Albert Grandolini Collection)

troops at some distance around their major base, to make sure that none of the Carabineros would try to defend the constitutional rule.

Within barely one hour, the whole of Chile was under the effective and overwhelming control of the military. The only place where any uncertainty remained was Santiago.[179]

Coup in Santiago

At 0630 hrs in the morning, Coloned Muñoz Conejeros Onesime, Deputy Director of the School of Carabineros in Norambuena, received a call from the prefect of Valparaíso, who announced that the Navy was taking over the control of the latter city. Onesime then made a call to Allende's residence in Tomás Moro Street to issue a warning. Immediately afterwards, he deployed four armoured cars with about 40 Carabineros to protect La Moneda. As soon as these arrived at the palace, Claudio Vengas Guzman, Chief of the Palace Guard, distributed them around the building.

At Allende's residence in Tomás Moro Street, the president appeared unsurprised by the news of the Navy's mutiny. He tried to call Montero on the telephone, but the line was cut: Leigh's whereabouts were unknown, while Pinochet was at home. Admiral Patricio Carvajal later observed that the delay with which the coup developed in Santiago confused Allende and convinced him that the military was active only in Valparaíso. Because of that the president went to La Moneda, and did not request a mobilisation of the industrial belts or communal commands.[180]

Before leaving his home, Allende phoned Joignant – the head of the police – and ordered him to take action against oppositional media, like the Radios Agricultura and Mineria, and the newspaper El Mercurio. Then, at 0715 hrs, he drove to La Moneda in a convoy escorted by four cars of the GAP, and Captain José Muñoz, a Carabinero who lead the presidential escort.

At 0700 hrs, General Javier Palacios boarded an armoured vehicle to harangue the troops of the 2nd Armoured Regiment in front of the commander of the unit, Alfredo Calderon. The unit then slowly moved out in the direction of the city centre. In order to avoid mistakes made by Souper, it split into two columns, which advanced along Amanategui and Bandera, and down the Agustinas Streets, until reaching Constitution Square. Three vehicles took positions directly around La Moneda, while others were positioned on the corners of Teatinos and Morandé Streets – and also to support the progress of troops from the Infantry School, which were late, and the artillery unit of Tacna. All the soldiers were advised to be careful not to open fire at friendly troops appearing from the south.[181]

At 0710 hrs, Allende's aide for the air force, Roberto Sánchez, arrived at the Ministry of Defence where he received the order to offer Allende an aircraft to leave the country as soon as possible.[182] Meanwhile, at Conception AB, three flights of four Hunters each from Grupos 7 and 9 were armed with Sura rockets. Among them were the following Hunters and pilots from Grupo 9:

- 702: Mario 'Libra' Lopez Tobar
- 712: Fernando Rojas Vendar (later C-in-C FACh)
- 711: Eitel von Mühlenbrock
- 704: Gustavo Leigh Yates
- 709: Ernesto 'Pekin' Gonzalez Yarra

Hunters from Grupo 7 known to have flown during the coup included serials J-722, J-726, and J-731. Their mission was to support the 'Silence Plan' – by bombarding the transmitters of government radios. Additionally, three Hunter FR.Mk 71As were to fly reconnaissance over Santiago and report the movement of people and vehicles.. Tobar took off first. At 0740 hrs, he attacked and destroyed Radio Corporacion's transmitter in La Florida, near

Row of Hunter fighter-bombers, at Concepción airfield, at 0600hrs of 11 September 1973. (FACh)

Vicuña Mackenna. After Mühlenbrok aborted prior to take off due to technical malfunction, the three other fighters attacked Colina and destroyed the radio transmitters of Pacifico and Luis Emilio Recabarren radios (curiously, the FACh failed to attack transmitters of the Magallanes and Corporation radio stations, though). Leigh's son rocketed Allende's home in eastern Santiago. For the Chilean air force, it was the first combat mission ever flown – and this was executed on the Chilean ground. Furthermore, it was not a particular success: at least one of younger Leigh's rockets hit the FACh Hospital, while another was so wide of its mark, it left a crater on the ground a few blocks away from Allende's residence.[183]

Meanwhile, Allende arrived at La Moneda at 0730 hrs, accompanied by 23 people, and flanked by his advisers Garcés and Olivares. Everybody carried AK-47s, but there were also a small number of machine guns and two or three RPG-7s.[184] Once inside, they began burning documents according to their priority, while others took defensive positions, including all of the entrances. Another group of 8 GAP; armed with AK-47s and one RPG-7, and led by Manuel Cortés; entered the Building of Public Works in Morandé Street and took positions selected already months ago.[185] Their task was to delay the advance of any troops from the south, in order to buy time until the arrival of loyalist forces.

Shortly after, presidential secretary Osvaldo Puccio, his son, and the police inspector Juan Seoane (who led police protection services of the presidency), arrived at La Moneda, accompanied by 7 police officers that reinforced those already present. All together, they had 15 assault rifles, Browning pistols and one Colt Cobra revolver.[186]

The information they received was confusing and indicative of the mutiny being limited to the Navy only. Rumours about troop movements in the Santiago area and the noise of airborne Hunters seem to have had no decisive effects. In order to get an idea of the situation, Letelier decided to go to his ministry. However, he was arrested by the military shortly after and locked in the Tacna garrison – becoming the first high-ranking prisoner of the day.

Having received no news from Pinochet, Allende concluded that the General had been arrested.[187] Moments later José Maria Sepúlveda arrived to assure the president of the support of the Carabineros, while Joan Garcés was convinced that if the uprising was bigger than the *Tancazo*, ordering workers to concentrate in the factories would be a mistake. Instead of keeping them passive, it would be better to deploy them around the city and converge them to the centre: that would deny the coup the ability to spread quickly. Allende agreed with this analysis and called Figueora, president of the CUT, to ask him to mobilize the workers. Five minutes later, he recorded his first speech for the Corporacion, Magallanes and Portales radio stations:

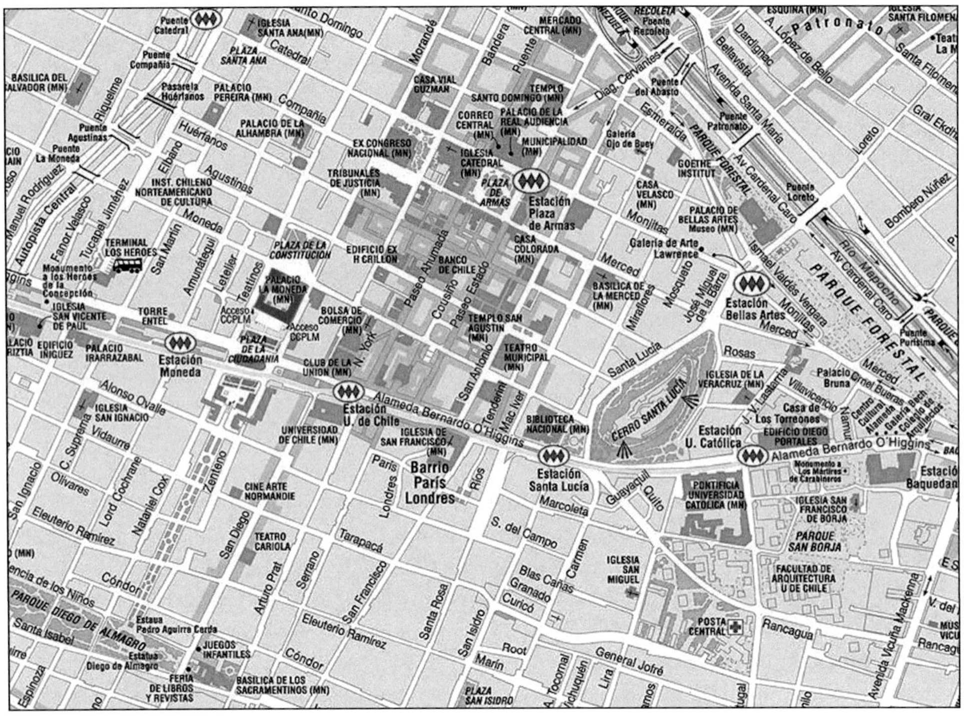

Plan of downtown Santiago, including La Moneda Palace (marked dark grey), and major public buildings nearby. (via Oscar Ruf Wilson)

Ministry of Public Works and Hotel Carrera, as seen on a postcard from the mid-1960s. (Mark Lepko Collection)

Colonel Medina Lois, who commanded a battalion of paratroopers that protected the HQ of the coup against Allende. (Albert Grandolini Collection)

A sector of the Navy has risen and the government is waiting to receive more information. What should workers do? Be attentive, vigilant and avoid provocations. As a first step, we must see the answer, which I hope will be positive, of the soldiers of the motherland who have sworn to respect the established regime.

Obviously, there was no talk about mobilisation of the Left or a march on the centre of Santiago.[188]

Meanwhile, Pinchoet arrived at the communication centre in Penalolén, which served as the headquarters of the plotters. The place was set up the day before by generals Benavides and Arellano, and protected by a battalion from the School of Paratroopers, commanded by Colonel Alejandro Medina Lois. Penalolén had no direct communication link with other branches of the armed forces. To remedy this issue, technicians had designed a network of telephone links, whose heart was in the Defence Staff – only to discover, during the morning of 11 September – that they could not communicate with the Air Warfare Academy. Overall, Pinochet (at Post 1) was only able to contact Leigh (at Post 2) via Carvajal (Post 5), or via the radio station of the Military Academy (Post 3), whose operator was an 18-years-old cadet.[189] Based at the Military Defence, Carvajal was at the heart of the action, and the only one to know all three commanders-in-chief. In another office on the same floor, General Herman Brady (Commander of the 2nd Division) and Arellano (Commander of the Centre Group) were posted, together with several civilians responsible for broadcasting the proclamation of new regime to the media.[190]

By 0800 hrs, Allende was still convinced that the coup only included parts of the Navy – a version he maintained during his second speech that morning, transmitted by Radio Magallanes. Therefore, he decided to gather forces and called the vice president of the CUT, Rolando Calderon, to ask him for measures taken by that group in the case of a military mutiny. Calderon replied that the union had planned the occupation of the factories, but did not know if this was done. Next, Allende asked Calderon to locate Prats, known to have spent the night at his daughter's house. However, nobody could find him because during the morning of 11 September, the former C-in-C of the Chilean military asked the son of his friend, General Ervaldo Rodriguez, to shelter him in his father's empty apartment. This removed Allende's hope that Prats might take over the command of the army and rally at least some units behind the government.[191]

Meanwhile, the Ministry of Defence – held by coup plotters – made a call to the aide-de-camp of the president, Roberto Sanchez, informing him that General Van Schouwen proposed to provide him with a DC-6 aircraft that would fly him out of the country. Allende flatly refused. Next, the president learned that Joignant and his deputy, Samuel Riquelme (who was a communist), had abandoned the police headquarters carrying away some weapons. Allende was furious that the two men had abandoned a force that was always loyal to the government.[192]

The situation thus began to darken for Allende: the Navy and the Air Force were in mutiny, and probably supported by some units of the Army. The position of the Carabineros was ambiguous, and the 3,000 police-officers were without leadership. Still, the president was hoping that at least some of generals – Pinochet for example – would remain loyal.

The streets of downtown Santiago were still full of civilians when the first tanks passed by in the direction of Moneda. (Albert Grandolini Collection)

Blockade of La Moneda

At 0842 hrs, Lieutenant-Colonel Guillard read a proclamation on the radio stations Mineria and Agricultura, which demanded that Allende hand over his powers to the High Command of the Chilean military and the Junta, including Pinochet, Leigh, Merino and Mendoza.[193] Furthermore, Guillard announced that if La Moneda did not surrender by 1100 hrs, it would be subjected to attacks 'from land and the air'. While this proclamation caused some surprise even within the ranks of the plotters – because nobody planned an aerial bombardment of the palace – it caused a severe shock in La Moneda because it made it obvious that the worst-case scenario was unfolding. Allende thus not only learned about Pinochet's betrayal, but realized that the only hope remaining was a possible division within the military, perhaps a fight between some of the involved units, and thus a civil war. Correspondingly, the president quickly prepared his third speech.

Unknown to Allende, Carabineros were involved in the coup too. Some of them reached the downtown using civilian cars. (Albert Grandolini Collection)

The situation at the palace became tense. Three generals of the Carabineros; Urrutia, Alvarez, and Salinas arrived, discouraged and depressed: most of their troops had changed their attitude and instead of protecting La Moneda de-facto besieged it. Unsurprisingly, Allende's relatives found it very difficult to reach the place. Isabel, the president's daughter, had to give up her weapon and identification papers in order to enter.[194]

Chilean Army troops moving in direction of La Moneda Palace on a Land Rover armed with a 107mm recoilless rifle. (Albert Grandolini Collection)

At the corner of Moneda and Morandé Street, a white car carrying Allende's secretary, Payita, his son, and Domingo Blanco (one of GAP's commanders), followed by a red truck that was carrying additional fire-arms from the Tomás Moro residence, were stopped by Carabineros and all occupants were arrested.[195] Payita subsequently managed to escape and return to the palace, only to find out that Urrutia was complaining that his men didn't obey his orders any more. When Beatriz Allende arrived, her father asked her to call the Cuban Embassy and order them not to go to La Moneda: in the president's opinion, this was a purely Chilean conflict, and he did not want to provoke a battle between the Cubans and the Chilean military.[196] Around the same time, Miguel Enríquez called Allende with an offer to join him, but the president responded that the MIR should fight on the streets instead – which Enríquez promptly promised to do.

Meanwhile, the few light armoured vehicles of the Carabineros began to leave, as did all the guards that were still outside the palace: only carabineros inside La Moneda remained at their posts. When Minister Jaimé Toha pointed out these departures, Allende went out to the balcony of his office – prompting an applause from onlookers standing at the Morandé Street. The president greeted them and a few journalists at the Constitution Square before returning inside and asking Sepúlveda about the meaning of the Carabineros' departure. The general was only able to reply that the central communications service was in the hands of the plotters, that the units probably received orders from there, and that he lacked men to take this crucial installation back.[197]

At 0900 hrs, Allende called General Baeza, at the Ministry of

An Army machine-gunner positioned opposite of the Building of Public Works, where a group of GAPs took positions. (Albert Grandolini Collection)

This military truck carrying troops approached La Moneda around 09:50, de-facto signalling the start of the attack on the palace. (Albert Grandolini Collection)

One of three M41 tanks that approached La Moneda around 1000 hrs. (Albert Grandolini Collection)

Troops taking position around one of three M41s deployed near La Moneda, as they came under fire from the group of GAPs positioned inside the Building of Public Works. (Albert Grandolini Collection)

Defence, on the telephone to tell him he did not accept the Junta's ultimatum, and did not believe the military would bomb La Moneda. Instead, he proposed a meeting at the High Command and negotiations to solve the crisis. Baeza replied that he had to ask for an agreement with Pinochet, who in turn replied that there was no time to organize such a meeting.[198]

Immediately afterwards, Allende prepared his next public speech – around the same time a Hunter, flown by Commander Tobar, made a reconnaissance pass over Santiago at an altitude of about 20,000ft.[199] Although the president was meanwhile conscious of his position, he failed to make it clear what he expected the workers and the population in general to do. In his next message, broadcast by Radio Magallanes at 0910 hrs, he de-facto improvised a farewell from the Chilean people by transmitting a vague message of restraint and resilience:

> You must not let yourself be provoked, do not let yourself be slaughtered, but you must also defend your conquests. You must defend the right to build your own efforts, a dignified and better life…These are my last words, and I am certain that my sacrifice will not be in vain. I am sure that, at the very last, it will be a lesson, that morality will punish crime, cowardice, and treason.200

Minutes later, Allende received a call from Admiral Carvajal, who informed him that the Junta refused a meeting at La Moneda. Instead, Carvajal repeated the offer for Allende to resign and take an aircraft that would fly him abroad. The president's three aides reiterated to him that a DC-6 was ready at Los Cerrillos, and emphasised the cooperation between the military and the Carabineros, thus making a civil war impossible. Allende responded with refusal to resign and announced he would kill himself in the palace.[201]

Meanwhile, the situation in Penalolén remained one of confusion because nobody knew what exactly was happening inside La Moneda. Rumours began circulating that Allende has committed suicide, but Carvajal responded that the president was still alive and had refused to surrender. Correspondingly, the admiral requested the Carabineros leave La Moneda, announcing that this would be bombed. Only then did Pinochet reply that the palace would be bombed at 1100 hrs, after which the Buin Regiment and the troops of the Infantry School would assault the place.[202]

Throughout this time, the radio stations controlled by the plotters began airing requests for the public to maintain order, warnings against acts of sabotage, and then a warning about a pending attack on La Moneda. Furthermore, the speakers requested that workers remain at their places of work, or face reprisals. Another message announced the imposition of martial law and a curfew starting at 1800 hrs: anybody encountered on the streets after this time would be shot on the spot.

Last Ditch Defence

Understanding that the palace was about to be attacked, Paredes prepared a plan to exfiltrate Allende. Four of the GAP were to surround the president (Juan Osses on his left, Osvaldo Ramos on the right, Jaime Sótelo and Juan José Montiglio behind), and bring him to the Ministry of Public Works in Morandé Street. The GAP group there was to support them: snipers were to take positions on the windows, and keep the army troops down, while Daniel Gutiérrez would deploy his RPG-7 against any armoured vehicles. From there, Allende was to be brought to the State Bank, across the street, and then down the

Carabineri leaving La Moneda with 'white flags', around 1030 hrs. Minutes later, the M41 tank deployed on Morandé Street opened fire at the palace. (Albert Grandolini Collection)

10:30 hrs: the M41 tank deployed on Morandé Street, soon followed by the soldiers deployed around it, began firing its machine gun at the palace. (Albert Grandolini Collection)

Bandera Street, where Juilo Soto would wait for him in a car. Once outside the immediate danger, the president was to be brought to the Indumet company, where 400 workers were supposed to protect him, or he would find refuge in a factory such as Sumar or Madeco. However, Allende flatly refused such an operation.[203]

Around 1000 hrs, the first shots were fired near La Moneda. These were the result of skirmishes between snipers of the GAP and troops who attempted to approach; the crew of a FACh helicopter circling downtown Santiago had shot a sniper positioned on the roof of Carrera Hotel.[204] Captain Escalona also recorded a total of 10 gun-shots at the Ministry of Defence. General Palacios then ordered his tanks to deploy around the palace, with three of these moving in its immediate vicinity, while additional vehicles approached from the south. Such manoeuvring caused a reaction from the GAP-group posted in the Building of Public Works: their shots stopped the advance of the troops commanded by Colonel Canessa, who had to take refuge under the doors of the Continental Theatre, and order his men to take cover. On the northern side of La Moneda, troops of the Infantry School, Armoured, and Tacna Regiments were sprayed by bullets fired from the Ministry of Finances, the newspaper La Nacion, the Central Bank, and the Workers Insurance Building. However, the defenders were too few to establish a continuous perimeter around La Moneda, and thus several routes of approach remained open. Furthermore, the troops poured ever increasing volumes of fire in return – even if none of them had shot directly at the presidential palace by that moment in time.[205]

Allende's Farewell

At 1015 hrs, at La Moneda, Augusto Olivares announced that Radio Magallanes was ready to broadcast a new message by Allende. In his final speech, the president spoke about 'moral punishment' against the leaders of the coup, announced that he would 'pay with life his loyalty to the people', and expressed gratitude to those, 'who will be prosecuted'.[206] Applying all of his oratory skills, he delivered a lyrical text that turned towards the future, announcing a defeat, but a glorious defeat on the condition there would be no unnecessary blood that would stain his memory.

Immediately afterwards, Allende gave Sepúlveda the freedom to retire, but the latter preferred to stay inside the palace. Then the president summoned Captain Muñoz from the Carabineros to tell him that his men were free to leave, but had to abandon their arms. The captain presented his helmet to Allende – the one that the latter would be seen wearing for the rest of the morning.

Immediately afterwards, and without Muñoz being informed, Yovane ordered the 48 Carabineros still present in La Moneda to 'leave as soon as possible'. Some left through the door on Teatinos Street, while others – including Muñoz – gathered at the front door, one of them holding a white flag. This group crossed Constitution Square and took refugee in an underground car park. Allende then summoned Inspector Seoane and allowed him to go, too. However, the valiant police officer refused to go: instead, he deployed 16 other inspectors for the defence of the palace.[207]

At 1030 hrs, without any kind of warning, the M41 tank deployed on Morandé Street opened fire at La Moneda, spraying windows on the first floor with machine gun fire. Several additional tanks followed in fashion; they were then joined by troops and Carabineros. Thus began the final assault on the presidential palace.

Allende reacted by meeting his remaining defenders at the Toesca lounge, announcing to them that a military coup was underway, and that nobody was on the side of the government. He thanked his followers, asked those that had children and the remaining six women – including his two daughters – to leave. Everybody sang the national anthem and then Allende saluted them, one by one. The medical team was to leave too, but Dr Victor Guijon refused to do so.[208]

Bombing of La Moneda

The Hawker Hunters of the Fuerza Aera de Chile were late. Despite Pinochet and Carvajal's orders, they proved unable to attack La Moneda at 1100 hrs, because they spent most of the morning flying reconnaissance and attacks on various points around the country. Around 1030 hrs, they were all ordered to land at Los Cerillos AB, refuel and re-arm. In an attempt to calm down an impatient Leigh, the C-in-C FACh announced that they would be ready for the next mission in 15 minutes. Actually, it took their ground crews about 40 minutes to turn them around.

With the Hunters being late, Pinochet ordered Brady to concentrate all the firepower of his tanks, APCs, and artillery on La Moneda. During the following 30 minutes, the northern front of the palace was showered with a rain of more than 50 shells. GAP's Antonio Aguirre deployed his machine gun on the balcony on the second floor to return fire, but his position was saturated by return fire and he was hit by several bullets.[209]

Inside La Moneda, José Toha called Badiola on the telephone, asking him to demand more time to enable him to convince Allende to surrender. Carvajal forwarded this proposal to Pinochet, but the latter refused. Carvajal then asked whether the offer to provide an aircraft for Allende's escape was still valid, which Pinochet answered in the affirmative – though with observation that the aircraft would

One of the Hunters that rocketed La Moneda around the noon, pulling up after its attack. (Albert Grandolini Collection)

An R80 rocket, fired by a Hunter, hitting the main door of the La Moneda palace, around 1152 hrs. (Albert Grandolini Collection)

Repeated rocket attacks on the palace set several parts of the building on fire. (Albert Grandolini Collection)

'fall in flight'.

Other senior officers attempted to convince Allende to demand a cease-fire, but he refused. They continued negotiations with the help of the telephone, and agreed to send a car for Sepúlveda, so he could negotiate instead. Yovane thus deployed three of the police's armoured vehicles on Morandé Street: these picked up Sepúlveda and brought him to the Officers' Club of the Carabineros.

Around 11:50, two Hunters finally appeared in the skies over the Chilean capital. They thundered from north to south, in the direction of La Moneda, breaking the sound barrier before turning left and returning north, never approaching less than one kilometre from the palace. Nevertheless, their mock attack prompted those still inside the palace to rake refugee from the incoming bombardment.

The Hunters came back two minutes later. This time their leader approached La Moneda and fired three rockets. These hit the main door and the offices on the first floor. Six seconds later, the wingman fired his rockets into the rooftop of the second floor. On the other side of the city, ambassador Davis' wife was monitoring the drama:

'It was an incredibly beautiful sight as they came out of nowhere. The sun glinted on their wings. There were only two. Still in formation, they climbed gracefully across the sky in a great circle, then they tipped and dove... a bomb each... then, a gentle curve upwards...'[210]

Two minutes later, the two Hunters returned to re-attack – this time from a more suitable angle. Their rockets hit the part of La Moneda between the Patios of Canones and Naranjos. The third attack followed another five minutes later: this time one of the rockets bounced off a gargoyle at the front of the palace, and exploded inside the 2nd floor of the south wing, inside the offices of the Chancellery. This hit caused a fire that slowly spread along the front of the palace.

At 12:08, the Hunters delivered their fourth attack, hitting the front of the palace with shells from their 30mm cannons, and setting the presidential flag on fire. The ensuing fireball set a vehicle parked nearby on fire. After this last pass, a strange silence followed, while La Moneda burned.[211]

Realising the Hunters were away, the defenders of the palace reorganised. No fewer than 67 people gathered in the northern wing – centre of the attack – including 20 officials, 15 police officers, 8 doctors, and 24 GAP; a group of nine found refuge in the south-western wing. The palace was meanwhile afire and, although appearing indestructible from the outside, to those inside it looked as if on the verge of collapse.[212]

Seeing no sign of surrender from La Moneda, General Baeza suggested the use tear gas, against the defenders, to Brady and Arellano. In a few minutes, the soldiers threw grenades on the rooves and terraces. The gas added to the smoke, causing an impression of suffocation inside the palace. The number of available gas masks was insufficient and Allende requested these to be used only by those with breathing difficulties. Because of the smoke and gas, the defenders moved towards windows, and resumed the fight from there. While Allende was searching for a good firing position on the second floor, three GAP operatives entered the Guards' Office on the corner of Moneda and Morandé Street, from where they were able to stop the advance of the troops outside.

La Moneda was meanwhile subjected to attacks from multiple directions:

- Two M41s approached from Teatinos Street, using their cannons as they went;
- From the south, troops of the NCO schools approached the palace

Top view of a FACh Hunter F.Mk 71A, showing details of national insignia and the way serials were applied. According to most of the available reports, all such markings were removed from the 12 aircraft deployed to attack various targets in and around Santiago on 11 September 1973. (via Santiago Rivas)

supported by the guns of the Tacna Regiment, positioned in the Alameda Street;

- Another column of troops – led by Sergeant Ramon Toto, a specialist in urban warfare – attempted to cross Lord Cochrane Avenue to the north sidewalk of Alameda Street. However, upon crossing the main avenue of Santiago, his soldiers came under deadly fire from the GAP snipers deployed inside the Ministry of Public Works.[213]

Battle for Tomás Moro Street

At 08:00 AM, at the Military School, General Benavides – the head of the Military Institutes – gathered his men to announce that the FF. AA was in the process of overthrowing the government. Their mission was to ensure order and to destroy the resistance attempts in their area of operation that included the north of Santiago and the vast eastern area. Benavides also had the task of seizing the residence of Tomás Moro. In the president's home, when the Carabineros bus arrived to take over protection, the GAP warned that they would not allow this to take place and let the Carabineros leave. There were no policemen to protect Tomás Moro's villa. Nevertheless the military acted with caution because, according to the services of military intelligence, the residence was a base of paramilitary instruction. The plan to seize Tomás Moro's villa therefore provided for its bombing by the FACh.[214]

A group of GAPs tried to organize the defence. They were joined by an officer from the special operations department of the Cuban army who was unable to reach his embassy. They were also joined by a dozen men from El Cañaveral. The shooters stood in the garden armed with AK-47s, and a machine gun was located in a small tower in the convent that adjoined the back of the house. They formed the outer line of defence against the troops of the Military School, and the Carabineros who arrived around noon and took refuge in the adjacent streets while the police circled the sector.[215] The assault on the residence would not be easy. The soldiers asked for air support, but this proved anything other than easy because of the lower cloud ceiling in the area than over the centre of the capital. Correspondingly, the order was issued for an air strike by two Hunters from Concepción to be guided by a helicopter piloted by Lieutenant Avila.

Avila approached Tomás Moro Street to fix the targets – only to find himself confronted by a hail of fire from automatic weapons. After three attempts to take a closer look at the target, he decided to withdraw. The defenders quickly changed position by the time the two Hawker Hunters appeared from the west. The first missed its target, and its rockets hit the 2nd floor of the nearby FACh hospital, injuring 14 people. The second hit the roof of the residence though. Driver Carlos Tellos then prepared a car that allowed Allende's wife, Hortensia Bussi, to visit the economist Felipe Herrera. There, she made contact with the Mexican ambassador who offered his protection for her to refuge in the Mexican Legation in the afternoon.[216]

At 12:45, the men of the GAP, who had two wounded, gathered in the garden of the ruined residence. Shortly before the bombing, on the orders of Arnoldo Camu, the GAP weapons were collected to be taken to Barros Luco Hospital. The vehicle was caught in the chaos of the bombing and the driver became aware that he could not fulfil his mission.[217] The GAP commanders did not expect an assault after the bombing because they didn't see any troops around the residence. Seeing this as a good opportunity to flee, the GAPs ran to the vehicles – including the one full of arms, and the presidential ambulance – and then quickly dispersed into the city, to avoid being tracked by helicopters. However, all their subsequent attempts to contact one of the leaders of the socialist militant apparatus proved unsuccessful.[218]

Surrender

By 1300 hrs, the situation inside La Moneda was deteriorating rapidly. Journalist Augusto Olivaro used his Uzi machine gun to shoot himself. Allende and the doctors came running, but could do nothing to save him: Olivaro died soon after, his death superimposing a sinister atmosphere in the darkened palace full of smoke, and prompting even Allende to start considering a surrender.[219]

Correspondingly, Minister Flores called the Ministry of Defence at 1315 hrs, and proposed surrender. Baeza and Carvajal agreed to send a military vehicle to pick up the negotiators – including Flores, Vergara and Puccio. Recovering his composure, Allende refused to negotiate, but at the same time listed his conditions: an end of bombardment, constitution of a military government without civilians, and maintenance of the 'social conquests' of the UP. At the Ministry of Defence, Carvajal, Leigh and Pinochet discussed the situation, and agreed that only Allende would be allowed to leave, together with Puccio: everybody else was to be arrested.[220]

Shortly after 1400 hrs, an M3 half-track approached the front of La Moneda to fetch Puccio, Vergara and Flores, and bring them to Carvajal's office. Immediately afterwards, fighting at the palace resumed, while ceilings began to collapse and the fire continued to spread.

Around this time, Seoane received a call from René Carrasco in the Police HQ: the latter was appointed by the Junta as the head of police and offered a cease-fire in order to enable defenders to surrender. Seoane immediately informed Paredes, who spoke to Allende, and the latter agreed. Paredes and Allende then warned the staff of this decision, and announced that while Payita would come out first, the president would follow as the last. Correspondingly, Paredes called Baeza to ask for a cease-fire and a car for Allende. Carvajal forwarded this message to the Junta, which reacted with another request for an unconditional surrender. Allende, his family, Puccio, Briones and Letelier could leave the country, but all others were to be arrested. Indeed, as soon as the Junta learned about the president's decision to surrender, it ordered his three negotiators to be arrested.[221]

Now it rested upon on General Palacios to reach La Moneda and receive the surrender. Carvajal attempted to de-conflict by radioing a broadcast about Allende's surrender, but the GAP continued firing at the troops in Alameda and Morandé Streets. Left without a choice, Palacios then ordered his tanks to spray the building with machine-

The M41 parked in Morandé Street continued pouring fire into the presidential palace after the air strike. (Albert Grandolini Collection)

This M41 and a group of troops approached the rear entry to La Moneda palace. (Albert Grandolini Collection)

Riddled by rockets and bullets, much of La Moneda was on fire by 1300 hrs. (Albert Grandolini Collection)

One of the last photographs of Allende, armed with an AK-47 and wearing a steel helmet while surrounded by his bodyguards of the GAP. (Albert Grandolini Collection)

gun fire. Only this action forced the GAPs to change their positions and decreased the intensity of the battle.[222]

Next, Palacios decided that it was time to assault and seize La Moneda. Correspondingly, he deployed a group of troops to knock the door on Morandé Street. They found this open. Inside were doctors Soto and Bartulin, a journalist, two GAPs and a police officer that approached the door with a white flag. The troops pulled them outside and forced them to lie on the street with their faces down. One of the officers then asked Soto to re-enter La Moneda and tell those still inside that they had 10 minutes to leave.[223]

Meanwhile, the remaining survivors lined-up on the second floor in preparation for an evacuation. Soto ran into this group and was surprised to find the president shaking hands and saying good-bye to every single one of his companions. He then asked them to leave their weapons and go downstairs, announcing he would follow as the last. However, as his aides left, Allende went to the Independence Lounge, and Enrique Huerta heard him – or thought he heard him – say, 'Allende does not surrender!'[224]

Doctor Guihon ran towards the Independence Lounge when he heard a shot: upon entering, he saw that Allende had shot himself in the chin. Reacting mechanically, he took president's pulse, as David Garrido and Enrique Huerta arrived.[225]

General Palacios meanwhile crossed Morandé Street. Armed with a machine gun, he passed by the group of prisoners gathered on the western sidewalk, to enter the still burning palace with the goal of finding Allende. He rushed upstairs only to come under fire from a GAP who was unaware of the order to surrender – and was promptly injured by ricocheting round in the hand. In an adrenaline-rush, Palacios continued examining all of the rooms until a soldier told him that a body had been found in the Independence Lounge. Finally there, the General found Doctor Gihon next to president's body, questioned him briefly without thinking much of it, and then called General Nuno on the radio, to issue a brief report:

> Mission accomplished, Moneda taken, president dead.[226]

At 1438 hrs, Carvajal informed Pinochet and Leigh.

Mop-Up

Outside La Moneda, troops pushed and kicked the survivors as they came out. Nearby, an M41 tank surrounded by conscripts, continued to fire at the Building of Public Works, from where shots were still being fired. The tankers then threatened to roll over the prisoners if the shooting did not stop, and the caterpillar began to move in the same direction. Despite the noise, the remaining GAPs understood what was going on and gave up. At 1430 hrs, the eastern wing of La Moneda was searched by Palacios and his troops, while in the West

Countless holes in the façade of La Moneda bear witness to the ferocity of the attack upon the palace. (Albert Grandolini Collection)

Near the rear entry to La Moneda, Army troops lined up everybody who exited the palace and forced them to lie on the ground. For a while the military threatened to crush the captives with the M41, visible in the background, if the last of Allende's defenders would not give up. (Albert Grandolini Collection)

As ever-more people exited the palace, the line of those forced to lie on the ground near the rear entry into La Moneda continued to grow. It was only during the evening that they were bussed away: most of them were never seen again. (Albert Grandolini Collection)

Army troops and firefighters carried the lifeless body of President Allende out of La Moneda palace. (Albert Grandolini Collection)

Captives were forced to board buses that took them to different detention centres. Most of them were summarily executed. (Albert Grandolini Collection)

At 1800 hrs, the four top commanders of the Chilean Armed Forces met at the Military School in Santiago, to officially take power of the country. (Albert Grandolini Collection)

Lieutenant Ramirez and a platoon of troops from the NCO School cautiously opened the door on Teatinos Street. Although fearing an ambush, they continued their progress until running into José Toha and two police officers before reaching the centre of the palace.[227] Palacios then decided to transfer all the prisoners to the Ministry of Public Works, and called in a group of experts, and a photographer from *El Mercurio*, to examine and photograph Allende's body.

Inside the Building of Public Works, the leader of the GAP group recognized that the fight was over and ordered his operatives to retreat. The eight men concealed their firearms within the ducts of the air conditioning and then joined the civil servants on the first floor. Palacios then ordered his troops to enter and evacuate the building: the GAPs came out first, all with false papers in their hand, which helped them pass through military controls without much difficulty: the troops were convinced that all of the snipers were still on the upper floors and the roof of the building. The GAPs thus came out, entirely free, of the building that proved to be the last bastion of resistance in the centre of Santiago.[228]

Around 1600 hrs, at the request of Leigh, the radio announced that for any soldier that was killed in a leftist attack, five Marxist prisoners would be shot. Immediately afterwards, he ordered Allende's body to be examined by four military doctors and the top medical examiner of Santiago, while General Bonilla proposed a military inquiry into the circumstances of the president's death. Two hours later, as the curfew took hold, two criminal police inspectors, accompanied by five

The military quickly set up dozens of checkpoints around Santiago. (Albert Grandolini Collection)

Soldiers searching for snipers positioned high in the surrounding buildings. (Albert Grandolini Collection)

crime experts, entered the Independence Lounge. Their findings left no doubt and remain valid until today: Allende committed suicide. The president's body was then taken way on a stretcher and brought to the Military Hospital; as buses arrived to drive the prisoners from Morandé Street to the Tacna Garrison. Calm gradually returned to the ruined La Moneda, although isolated shots were heard throughout the following night around Santiago.

At 2100 hrs, an autopsy of Allende's body was organized at the military hospital. The circumstances of his death made him an historical figure: for the next three decades his image would wander like an unburied ghost that would haunt his successors and the victors. The latter would secretly proceed to his burial – although they officially registered his death only two years later. Allende's private conduct would be denounced by slanders: his demonization was a reaction to fighting the image of a man who gave his life for his ideas. On the contrary, Allende's suicide became taboo for that part of the Left in the world who preferred to superimpose the image of a president who died in battle, with weapons in his hand. Castro looked for witnesses to prove that Allende died fighting. A GAP would assert that Allende was killed by a group of fascists under the command of a superior officer, which Castro repeated in his speech of September 28.[229]

Late in the evening of 13 September, buses brought the prisoners of La Moneda to the Tacna Regiment's base. They were herded inside the old stables and left lying on their hands. The next day, the policemen were released; while 24 prisoners were summarily executed in the Peldehue Military Base, after being forced to dig their own graves. Years later, their remnants would be removed and scattered in different places. The authorities then launched a cover-up and declared that Paredes died in a fire-fight, while in reality he was executed, just like Ricardo Pincheira, who was responsible for counter-intelligence for the PS – although the military did not know about his identity. Eleven other people were lined up and then summarily executed on Buelnes Bridge, and their corpses thrown in the Mapocho river to terrorize the population of Santiago[230].

CHAPTER 6

RESISTANCE TO THE COUP

The resistance to the military coup in Chile of 11 September 1973 was minimal and scattered. Some of leftist parties did attempt to mobilize their activists, but generally, their actions proved too little, too late, and much too disorganised but to pose any kind of a serious problem for the Junta that was in the process of taking over.

Reaction from the PS

During the morning, Altamirano, the Secretary General of the PS, met with 10 out of 13 members of the Central Committee of that party. None of them knew what was really going on, and all were convinced that the mutiny affected the Navy only. Nevertheless, they did decide to request Allende to leave La Moneda for a safer place, and start organizing resistance. Only after further deliberations did the leaders of the PS eventually decide to broadcast a call for mobilisation. However, the necessary radio transmitter was knocked out in one of the Hunter attacks.[231]

At the HQ of the PS, Senator Maria Elena Carrera and a group of activists were waiting for instructions. They developed a plan to deploy workers to seize bridges on the Mapocho River and thus block any threats from the north. However, they never received orders from top leaders of the party, and thus never did anything.

Members of the Special Support Group of the PS (*Grupo Especial de Apoyo*, GEA) met at the HQ of the Central Committee of the PS. However, they not only lacked arms but also had no orders. When somebody suggested them that they go to La Moneda, the GAP leader in situ, Sótelo, ordered them to disperse instead, burn the party's archive, find a refuge and reorganize later. Despite the optimism of those around him, Sótelo seems to have correctly predicted a victory of coup plotters.[232] Eight members of this group left in three cars for Mademsa in hope of finding Altamirano: all ended isolated in an industrial zone.

At 0950 hrs, Hernan del Canto visited Allende in La Moneda together with the head of the Counter-Espionage Party of the PS, Ricardo Pincheira. Arriving there, the two found the palace already buzzing with rumours and the GAPs and police officers standing guard along windows on both floors. Canto demanded that Allende inform the PS about the military situation, expressed his will to fight in the president's defence, and requested him to leave the palace. Explaining that his role as president was to stay on the spot, Allende refused, leaving Canto little choice but to drive to the CORMU Stadium, where he called the Central Committee of the PS and warned everybody to avoid the centre of Santiago.[233]

Elsewhere around Santiago, various leftist leaders attempted to mobilise the local industrial belts. However, when activists attempted to reach the CORMU Stadium they – just like Altamirano and Sepúlveda – encountered numerous military patrols, armoured vehicles, artillery, and airborne helicopters. Finally understanding that this was not a small scale mutiny but a major blow, they concluded that armed resistance made no sense, and retreated. Curiously, although it finally dawned upon the leaders of the PS that La Moneda was the centre stage of the unfolding drama, none of them made a call to warn Allende.[234]

Meanwhile, about 150 activists of the GEO did manage to gather at the CORMU Stadium, and their leaders developed a four-stage plan, including the gathering of available forces in southern Santiago (especially in the San Miguel area, but also around San Joaquin and Vicuña Mackenna), establishment of a free zone, and then a march to the centre of the capital and support of Allende at La Moneda. This operation was to be coordinated with similar actions of the UP and the MIR. However, the activists were forced to realise that they only had about 120 AK-47s and 4 RPG-7s, which was clearly insufficient to face the military might already deployed inside Santiago.[235]

Indecisiveness at Indumet

Eventually, the gathering at the CORMU Stadium split into two major groups: about 100 activists led by Arnolod Camú left in a convoy of cars and trucks in direction of the Indumet industrial complex. Others remained on the spot, still waiting for instructions from the PS leadership.

In Indumet, Camú's group found 86 workers, most of them trained in the use of fire arms. The factory manager, Socrates Ponce (a lawyer and economist) then gathered everybody to announce that the military had launched a coup and that the local metallurgical centre was the centrepiece of defence of the government. He offered those who did not want to fight the opportunity to leave. Nobody moved.[236]

However, while Indumet was a good place to hide and store arms and ammunition (because of its extensive underground facilities), its choice as a gathering area was not the best. The main access was through the narrow Rivas Street: this made the surveillance easy, and offered good opportunities for blocking the approach, but also meant that the exit was easy to block, too. Around 1000 hrs, supplies for about a week for 400 men arrived: this was how long the activists expected their showdown with the military to last, before they could launch their counteroffensive.

By 1245 hrs, there was feverish activity in Indumet, as operators of the GEO, supported by a small group of the GAPs, began training workers on AK-47s and Walther sub machine guns. They were joined by the political committee of the MIR, including Miguel Enríquez and Victor Diaz (Deputy Secretary General of the PC), the former communist minister Oyarce, and several members of the Central Committee of the PS, including Canto.[237] However, members of the PCCh announced that their leadership had decided not to resist the coup. Actually, journalists of that party's newspaper, *El Siglo*, learned about the coup timely enough to warn their readers to 'move to fighting positions'. However, nobody had a trace of an idea where these should have been. Furthermore, it had become obvious that the military had taken control of all the country and that none of its elements sided with the government.[238]

The PCCh thus withdrew from the scene; the MIR struggled

The Junta deployed Carabineros and army troops to brutally suppress any kind of unrest in the population. (Albert Grandolini Collection)

The days after the coup of 11 September 1973 saw a campaign of arrest all over Chile: hundreds were detailed by Carabineros and army troops on the streets. (Albert Grandolini Collection)

trying to coordinate, arm and train its activists in a rush, while the PS remained paralysed by interrupted communications and the indecision of its leaders. The unsurprising result of the negotiations between leftist leaders that were present was disagreement. Stressing that the Secretary General of the PS ordered the withdrawal of its military wing, while Allende decided to stay at La Moneda no matter what happened, Canto concluded that there was no way to help anybody. Camú disagreed with this analysis, and called Paredes in La Moneda to find out what was going on. The latter informed him that the palace was under attack and the situation difficult, and that he waited for reinforcements.[239] Finally agreeing with Canto, Camú then broke with the line adopted by the PS' leadership and asked Miguel Enríques, leader of MIR's military wing, how his group could support the planned attempt to reinforce defenders of La Moneda. Enríquez replied that the Fuerza central was about to gather 50 well-trained men at 1600 hrs and that he was in the process of developing a plan for action. Along with the latter, the Fuerza GEO and the GAPs would advance through Santa Rosa, and the Fuerza central through San Diego and Arturo Prat with the aim of reaching Morandé Street under cover from the GAPs in the Building of Public Works.[240]

It was at this moment that one of the workers warned everybody that the factory was encircled by 'about 100 Carabineros' deployed in Nueva Macul, Santa Ana and Rivas Streets. Camú quickly moved out to organise defences: as the workers, GEOs and GAPs deployed, they came under fire, and began shooting back.[241] However, the longer the fire-fight continued the more the resistance began to crumble. Manuel

Outside a few areas still under control of leftist militants and activists, various 'security' forces moved quickly to find, arrest and take away dozens, then hundreds, and finally thousands of Chilean leftists. Many were never seen again. (Albert Grandolini Collection)

By the noon of 11 September 1973, troops of the Chilean military had surrounded Santiago and began treating its population like that of an occupied city. (Albert Grandolini Collection)

Ojeda was shot, while MIR leaders – convinced it was better for them to focus on clandestine work – fled out of the back of the factory. Under pressure, Camú then brought the decision to evacuate the rest of GEOs, GAPs, and workers and attempt regrouping in the Sumar Works, where up to 1000 additional activists had gathered. With this, he gave up the goal he had set for himself: providing support to Allende, besieged at La Moneda. Obviously, the fierce attack by the military had proved the coup plotter's strategy of demonstrating their readiness to apply violence as 'correct'.[242]

Intervention of the Carabineros

How did the Carabineros find out that Indumet was a gathering place for leftist militants?

A shopkeeper from one of nearby neighbourhoods called the police to announce the presence of a 'large armed group'. The Carabineros sent a patrol that was received with insults from the workers, and then somebody fired into the air. Left without choice, the Carabineros called for reinforcements. The contingent deployed initially was sufficient to besiege the Indumet complex for an indefinite period of time, but more Carabineros were to follow – even more so because the radio began airing fake news about Indumet's workers shooting their comrades. Before long their commanders also moved a contingent from the UTE University, and several Mowag armoured cars, towards Indumet. Once in place, one armoured car crashed through the main gate and, despite fierce fire from the entrenched workers, entered the

The entrance to the National Stadium, where thousands of detainees were concentrated for prosecution. Once brought there, they were forced to stand in front of a wall, hands behind their heads, all the time exposed to threatening shouts, kicks and blows. (Albert Grandolini Collection)

factory. By the time the second armoured car drove through the gate, the workers ceased firing: somebody then ordered them to drop their weapons, and they did as advised: a few rushed to a large pit where they used grease to remove traces of gun powder on their hands. Workers near the main gate raised a white flag and requested that the Carabineros cease fire.

As the Carabineros began gathering the workers in the yard of the factory, everybody came under fire from a socialist group that had escaped to the Plansa factory, and several of the soldiers were hit. The shooting stopped only around 1700 hrs, when militants left their positions. By 1845 hrs, the Carabineros secured the entire Indumet complex, lined up their prisoners and began loading them into buses that took them to the base of the Tacna Regiment.[243] With this, the Left had lost the only place where it had a serious chance of organizing armed resistance and a determined advance on La Moneda.[244]

Battle of La Legua[245]

Meanwhile, the small group led by Camú that had left Indumet via the Plansa factory, had crossed San Joaquin Avenue in a southern direction. On the other side of the avenue, they found themselves facing a big wall that surrounded two factories in the Venecia Alley. Although the situation appeared nearly suicidal, Camú ordered his militants to continue down the alley, with two men as a rearguard, about 20 metres behind the main group. What followed was a clear action motivated by desperation, without any kind of military-related rationale or revolutionary audacity: nothing but blind despair of people aware that Allende was fighting a desperate struggle in La Moneda. Namely, poorly armed militants had to cover more than three kilometres to reach the besieged palace. Even if, despite this obstacle, they could reach La Moneda, they would face about 2,000 heavily armed troops.[246]

Nevertheless, Camú's group continued. Leaving the Venecia Alley, it entered the La Legua district – an area populated by staunch supporters of Allende, who found the prospect of the government's fall outright unacceptable.[247] Much of the population was on the streets, women offering water and tea, and shelter inside their homes. Next, somebody informed them that a truck driven by a GAP operative was parked on the Guacolda Square – a junction of Los Copihues and Estrella Polar Streets. Although the vehicle contained only about 30 fire-arms, and very little ammunition, everybody rushed to arm himself.[248]

Before long, some of the militants in La Legua took positions on the rooftops of the Comandari Factory, from where they opened fire at

Terror at the scenes around him is clearly to be seen in the eyes of the detainee in the centre, Daniel Cespedes. He was one of the few that went through one of the Junta's concentration camps, and was tortured, but came away to tell his story. (Albert Grandolini Collection)

Army troops guarding leftist prisoners at the National Stadium, while the latter are waiting for their fate to be decided. (Albert Grandolini Collection)

the Carabineros besieging Indumet (only about 200 metres away), and at Police Station No. 22 in La Cisterna. Understanding the precarious position of the latter, Major Mario Salazar loaded 27 Carabineros into three vehicles and decided to take control of the Comandari Works. His vehicles entered La Legua from the south-eastern direction and passed by the GAP truck before coming under fire. With urgency, Salazar ordered his column into the Toro y Zambrano Street. However, only seconds later, as the vehicles reached the corner of Estrala Polar Street, all came under heavy fire from the front. The Carabineros debussed under a hail of bullets and took cover in the nearby buildings. Noting that the shots came from different places around him, including rooves, Salazar realized that he had been ambushed not only by socialist militants as he expected, but by local communist youth, too. Despite losing two killed, he managed to regroup his troops and evacuate six wounded to the Barros Luco hospital. Then the battle of La Legua began in earnest.[249].

At 1730 hrs, another bus of Carabineros approached the area where the first group was ambushed. Knowing what was awaiting them, the troops immediately returned fire and killed Francisco Cattani, a laboratory technician that was in the process of loading his RPG-7. A student next to him grabbed the launcher and fired, hitting the bus – but the rocket failed to detonate. With their vehicle riddled by bullets, the Carabineros disembarked and took positions along the street.

Nearby, another bus of Carabineros drove into a similar ambush and had its driver killed with the first volley of shots. The survivors took cover under their seats, receiving fire from all directions as the leftists kept on firing and moving all the time. Eventually, one of the Carabineros took the driver's seat and moved the bus to the Gran Avenida, eventually saving all the passengers.[250]

Southeast of La Legua, several groups of Fuerza GEO gathered for a march on the Sumar Factory. There, Renato Moreau – Camú's colleague – requisitioned a fire truck in support of his militants: that truck was to 'camouflage' them form the military, but also offer them greater mobility. Moreau used it to drive around and call the population to 'march on Sumar'. Not all the workers were in such high spirits, though. In the cotton factory, the leaders of the trade union rejected the idea of armed resistance and demanded that the workers go home. In the nearby polyester factory, drivers of two GAP vehicles distributed arms, and when an Aerospatiale SA.330 Puma helicopter of the FACh passed by, around 1530 hrs, it received 17 hits. As Camú's group withdrew from La Legua, its rear guard noticed an ambulance car of the carabineros arriving at Placa Guacolda. Thinking it was a ruse, the militants opened fire, drilling the vehicle with 32 hits.[251]

When Camú's group reached the Sumar Factory, around 1810 hrs, it found that out of nearly 1,000 workers that gathered there in the morning, only about 300 were still around. The rest – including the president of the local union – had all gone home. Realising that the people around them were in no fighting spirit, the militants decided to move to the Mercado Works, in El Pinar Street. As they were embarking about a dozen cars, an unarmed DHC-6 Twin Otter of the FACh passed overhead, prompting everybody to scramble for cover. Camús group thus dissolved on its own, with most of its militants, and dozens of accompanying workers, seeking refuge in nearby houses, from where they did not emerge for several days. What remained of the column ran into a patrol from the air force, and fled after only a short fire-fight. Only a small group reached the Madeco Works, where it was decided to abandon the idea of marching on La Moneda, disband and go into hiding.[252]

Some PS activists remained in La Legua for a few days longer, and a few skirmished with the police, Carabineros, and the military, time and again. Five days later, the Army encircled the neighbourhood before starting to raid it, arresting activists as it went. In the nearby town of El Pinar, it was the ground troops of the air force that accomplished a similar mission. Arnoldo Camú was arrested on 24 September 1973, while attending a meeting in Santiaguillo Street, during his efforts to rebuild the socialist apparatus. Police officers took him away in a car: his body was found only 15 days later by his brother David, and his father-in-law, Oscar Parrau.

Overall, nowhere was Allende's government defended as much as in La Legua. Clashes there resulted in six dead Carabineros and dozens of wounded civilians. The Junta's repression was correspondingly harsh: about 400 activists were arrested and detained at El Bosque AB and the National Stadium. According to historians of the National Commission for Truth and Reconciliation, at least 43 of these were summarily executed, and nine went missing.[253]

Siege of the Cuban Embassy

Just before 1800 hrs on 11 September 1973, Ulises Estrada, head of Chilean Operations at the DGLN, was informed of the coup by telephone. He immediately left for the Cuban embassy where he set off a series of phone calls around Santiago, transmitting the code word "lapis". This meant that a military coup was underway and Cubans had to leave their homes immediately. Estrada also alerted Altamirano and Samuel Riquelme, deputy chief of police. According to Estrada's memory, both had difficulty grasping the magnitude of what was happening[254].

The staff of the embassy was relatively well informed about developments during the day – thanks to telephone contact with

The siege of the Cuban embassy in Santiago began around the noon of 12 September, when about 200 Chilean troops surrounded the building. (Albert Grandolini Collection)

The Junta deployed at least one M41 tank near the Cuban embassy, 'should the need arise'. (Albert Grandolini Collection)

La Moneda, and offices of *Prensa Latina* in front of the palace. Unsurprisingly, about a hundred Cuban nationals gathered there by 0730 hrs. The building was blocked, weapons were distributed and most of the people inside – including 43 operatives of the DGLN – assumed defensive positions. While appearing a modest adobe house from the outside, for all practical purposes, the embassy was turned into a fortress awaiting siege. The building's pool had been concreted to conceal a water reservoir, and in a recently dug-out cellar the Cubans had stocked basic medical supplies to treat the wounded. In all, they calculated that they had provisions to last a month. As a part of sovereign Cuban territory, the place had to be defended.[255]

Around 1000 hrs, two unarmed members of the MIR – including Andres Pascal Allende, the president's nephew – managed to reach the embassy. When they arrived, they asked to receive at least some of the weapons promised by the Cubans. However, Estrada, who was actually in charge of the operations, thought it would have been "irresponsible". Estrada's decision was based on his fear that such weapons would be seized. It was only because the others didn't support this view that the two members of the MIR left the embassy with two pistols provided for self-defence.[256]

Around noon, about 200 Chilean troops surrounded the embassy, occupied the neighbouring buildings, and cut off all communications to the outside world. Estrada ordered that the embassy radio be destroyed in the event that the building would be invaded, and for all the documentation to be burned. Later on, Luis Fernandez Oña, DGLN member, also set fire to Allende's private papers in the backyard.[257]

From Penalolén, Pinochet called Carvajal to announce that the Cuban embassy had been surrounded and that a machine gun had fired on the soldiers. According to neighbours, two Cubans opened fire to intimidate them and the soldiers responded. To avoid a diplomatic incident, Pinochet put a plane at the disposal of the ambassador to leave the country, and announced that diplomatic relations would be broken. Carvajal also warned the ambassador that the Junta would not tolerate any kind of further attacks from within the embassy. Once again, the ambassador ordered his staff to prepare for defence.[258]

Around 2000 hrs, Oña – Beatriz Allende's husband – received a call from the Ministry of Defence informing him that his wife was wanted for Allende's funeral. He agreed, provided that Allende's daughters could ask for asylum in Cuba. The Junta replied positively. Oña and the ambassador wanted to go into the street to wait for the car that had to look for Beatriz. However, their exit provoked a violent exchange of fire. The Chilean military had been ordered not to allow anyone in or out, while embassy employees had orders to repel any attack. The shooting lasted a few minutes but ended without casualties.

Swedish ambassador Harald Edelstam appeared on the scene to announce that his country now represented Cuban interests in Chile. He opened negotiations with the Junta, resulting in the latter granting permission for the Cubans to leave the country. Isabel Allende, Carmen Paz, and their mother left the country under Mexican protection, on 15 September 1973.[259]

Losses suffered by the Chilean military during this affair remain unknown. Two Cubans – including their ambassador – were wounded.

The vindictive targeting of Cubans by the Chilean military and paramilitary forces revealed as much about their priorities as about their fears. Throughout 11 September, the Junta threatened to send tanks and fighters to bomb the embassy, while a Cuban merchant ship, *Playa Larga*, was intercepted and boarded while off Valparaíso. Starting with the next day, the embassy was put under an effective siege, but never came under an outright assault. In the end, everybody inside was left to go. Transcripts of Pinochet's conversations with the other leaders of the coup on 11 September reveal the reasons – foremost including Allende's ties with Cuba. Pinochet personally insisted on inserting a clause in the army's radio statement pointing to 'the aliens who murdered our people' and 'the foreigners who have intervened here on our territory'.[260]

In comparison, no other embassy faced similar pressure. The Soviet embassy was briefly surrounded on 12 September, but escaped the wrath of the military.

Other Centres of Resistance

At 6 PM, in the district La Victoria – south of the capital – Jorge Aravena, head of Socialist Youth, tried to cover the retreat of the inhabitants who gathered around his car in front of the irruption of troops of the FACh into the streets; this area had been known as "red" and combative since its creation in October 1957. Aravena, and the GAP Alejandro Cid, travelled through Santiago to join a combat post. They went to the police headquarters where Joignant gave them machine guns to get to La Victoria. In the neighbourhood, people were on the streets, anxious and waiting for instructions. When Aravena's car arrived, women offered drinks and men proposed to build barricades or dig trenches. It was at this moment that the soldiers came; Aravena shot for a few minutes before being killed. The soldiers invested the neighbourhood and shot here and there to frighten away the curious.[261]

In addition to the working class neighbourhoods, the military had paid special attention to the UTE, a Left stronghold. At 3:25 PM, a naval infantry patrol came to the door of the UTE rectorate where a Chilean flag flew at half-mast. A thousand students, teachers, officials

An Army patrol on the streets of one of the poorer neighbourhoods of Santiago, September 1973. (Albert Grandolini Collection)

as well as rector – communist Enrique Kirberg – remained on the campus formed of different buildings and gardens. They gathered because that day Allende was to have come on campus to give a speech and announce the referendum.[262]

At the announcement of the coup, the students and teachers of this "red" university decided to stay. Only the socialist group left with the aim of creating a pocket of resistance in the suburbs of José Maria Caro. The students witnessed the bombing of La Moneda from the buildings of the faculty, and at 1:30 PM the head of the student federation, the communist Ociel Nuñez, called the resistance, but students had no weapons or plans. With the naval infantry, the students also saw the arrival of the Carabineros' buses that blocked the access roads while dozens of others occupied the rooves of Villa Portales neighbour. Two hours later, the Carabineros warned that those who would not leave before the curfew at 6 PM would have to stay overnight, and at noon they would be taken by bus to return home. Nevertheless, most students decided to stay.

In the evening at the UTE, which has been surrounded since the afternoon, only a few hundred students remained. At the School of Art there were two machine guns on campus. It was impossible to know where the shooting began, which lasted for half an hour before midnight. Everything suggested that it was a cross-fire from the sailors posted at Quinta Normal north-west and soldiers to the south-west. The shooting stopped at the moment when a socialist photographer was mortally wounded in the School of Arts. The rector warned the Carabineros, but the ambulance could not enter the campus and those wounded died. The situation at the UTE reflected that of many places in Santiago: hundreds of people trapped in a compound that began to become a collective prison. The next day students and teachers of the UTE would meet at the Stadium of Chile, a mass detention centre, then came the National Stadium, Pisagua, Chacabuco, Ritoque, and Dawson.[263]

In the province of Valvidia, it was the MIR that led an episode of resistance against the coup and sought to organize a form of rural guerrilla warfare. The MIR developed in this region an embryonic rural *Fuerza central*, whose base was the agricultural complex of the Panguipulli forest. The leader of the group was a 28-year-old agronomist named Jose Gregorio Liendo Vera, better known by his combat name, "Commandante Pepe". On 11 September, when he learned of the coup, with about 200 men, and armed with an old Mauser rifle (which only had six bullets), dynamite sticks and Molotov cocktails, he tried to seize the Nelturne Carabineros post defended by five Carabineros under the control of Sergeant Benito Carrasco Riffo.

In the afternoon, Liendo met MIR activists. They made the decision to organize the siege of the post and wait for the surrender of the Carabineros and the outcome of the coup in Santiago. Towards evening, a call for surrender was greeted by shots from the Carabineros. Liendo's men responded with bullets and the shooting started. The fight remained indecisive, but in the darkness of the night a detachment of Carabineros burst through. They were attacked by the guerrillas who surrounded the barracks at the rear; a Carabineros patrol which was travelling in a jeep, managed to get into the combat zone because the guerrilla position on the access road hadn't opened fire: inexplicably, the militants let the vehicle pass. The arrival of more Carabineros surprised the attackers, who now came under fire from two directions. Thus, in the middle of the night, Liendo's men escaped in different directions. The next morning, pursued by police and soldiers, a group of guerrillas including Liendo, was arrested in the mountains before being able to cross the border and find refuge in Argentina. The new authorities accused them of attacking the Nelturne checkpoint; in accordance with the Valdivia War Council's judgment, Liendo was executed on 3 October 1973 with 10 other comrades.[264]

Change of Power in Santiago

In a single day the oldest democracy in Latin America disappeared. With it, the hopes of millions of people in Chile and around the world collapsed. Whose fault was it? There were many reasons for the 11 September coup, both in an international and national context. On the international level, Chile didn't escape the relentless logic of the Cold War. The election of Allende to the presidency of Chile provoked the anger of Washington which refused to allow the installation of a Marxist government in its sphere of influence. The Cuban precedent of 1959 reinforced this fear of a new advance of Soviet imperialism. Even though the socialist camp was friendly with Allende, *Détente* was on the agenda of the foreign policy of the USSR. There was no question of their provoking the anger of the United States, and Moscow was making that known in Havana. Nevertheless, opponents of the UP denounced the Soviet and Cuban influence behind Allende's plans while the Left denounced the American involvement. All this was true. The CIA paid millions of dollars to Chile while the Cubans offered their help, and the Soviet some credits. But Washington, Moscow and Havana played only a marginal role in the events leading up to 11 September, whose roots lied within Chile.

The traditional Right, represented by the PN, refused to recognize the democratic legitimacy of Allende, and only wanted to bring about his failure and the overthrow of the UP government. It put all of the means at its disposal into the service of this objective, before receiving the support of the PDC which participated in spreading terror among the population, mainly the middle class, in the face of Allende's policy. The PDC's refusal to reach a compromise with the president in the summer of 1973 accelerated the political crisis.

Splits within the Left also increased Chile's instability. The reformist line that represented Allende, and who wanted to be respectful of the legality and institutions, opposed a radical line that went beyond the framework of the UP to integrate the MIR. Altamirano, who represented this revolutionary line, imagined, like Castro, the struggle of Chilean socialism on the model of Vietnam. More concretely, they considered a Spanish-style situation, a civil war with the contribution of foreign volunteers, or that of Chile in 1891 with a divided army putting forward fanatical civilians. The evocation of Dien Bien Phu, Quang Tri, and the Vietcong militias were the expression of a revolutionary romanticism, but this inflamed rhetoric was also over-interpreted by some of the opposition and in the FF. AA. The PS systematically rejected Allende's moderate initiatives throughout 1973 and even the referendum, the last solution before the fire. It had constantly supported the formation of the Cordónes industriales,

As well as prosecuting any known or suspected leftist activists, in its efforts to 'cure the cancer of Marxism', the military went to great efforts to collect and destroy any leftist literature it could find. (Albert Grandolini Collection)

Actions against 'leftist propaganda' included the public burning of any of leftist literature captured during the many raids launched by the military and Carabineros in the aftermath of the coup. (Albert Grandolini Collection)

Carabineros watching the removal of political inscriptions on the walls of Santiago. (Albert Grandolini Collection)

The Arsenales de Chile, in Santiago, was also turned into a detention centre during the rule of the Junta. (Albert Grandolini Collection)

an expression of the discontent of the far left in the face of Allende's economic and social policy.

In a situation of political, social and economic chaos, the FF. AA had long supported Allende, even agreeing to participate in the government twice. Despite the proximity of some officers to the opposition and the extreme right, despite the importance of the doctrine of national security taught at the School of Americas, the FF. AA remained loyalists as evidenced by the isolation of units participating in the *Tancazo*. Nevertheless, this event provoked a shock in the Armed Forces. The speeches of not just Altamirano, but also those of Allende at that moment on the armament of the people, ended up convincing the military that behind the reassuring speeches of the president hid the will to form a popular army. Although the *Tancazo* was defeated by Prats' troops and not by "popular power," the UP parties then showed a tendency to want to establish a People's Army on the ruins of the old army, or to want rally the troops against their officers. For the armed forces, it was therefore a matter of survival that motivated their unanimous participation in the coup. This also explained the ferocity of the repression that was the counterpart to the experience of a deadly threat to the existence of the FF. AA. Even the CIA had acknowledged that the Junta had "planned" a "severe crackdown" to "permanently eradicate all vestiges of communism in Chile."[265]

The Armed Forces decided at this time to act to restore order, Allende having already appealed to them following the strike of October 1972 to stabilize the situation. But this time their intervention was against the president. To avoid a civil war, the plotters realized the unity of all branches of the armed forces. At this moment, Pinochet, perceived as an undecided commander, was removed from the action plans. It was only on 8 September that he was forced to participate in the coup.

On the evening of 11 September, members of the Military Junta, Pinochet, Leigh, Merino and Mendoza, met at the Military School. They talked on the need to maintain the state of siege, and discussed the likely rupture of relations with the Soviet bloc, but also debated how to announce the death of Allende. The agreement was to issue a statement, but to keep the burial place secret. To lead the Junta, they agreed on a rotating presidency that would start with Pinochet, then Merino, Leigh and finally Mendoza. Moments later, they were joined by the Brazilian ambassador since his country recognized the Junta as the legitimate government of Chile.

In the evening, on the cameras of the Canal 13 channel, the members of the Junta appeared on television for the first time. Each improvised a brief speech. Most of them were patriotic and moderate except Leigh, who denounced the "Marxist cancer". Colonel Montero then read Legislative Decree No. 1, which established a state of siege and swore an oath to Pinochet as President of the Junta[266]. The military dictatorship began.

It was also on the evening of 11 September that lists of the accused began to arrive in all the barracks. The violence came not only from the military, and affected the union leaders, workers and peasants whose destinies illustrate the hatred born of factory occupations or the expropriation of land during the agrarian reform. Civilians also took part; in addition to those who tracked down and liquidated 23 peasants from 3 settlements in Paine, civilian collaborators assisted the Carabineros in executing peasant leaders in Santa Barbara and workers in Quilaco; a civilian mounted patrol helped to shoot 18 agricultural workers in Mulchen; civilians made lists of peasants in Liquine who would be executed on a suspension bridge over the Pitrufquén river.[267]

The repression was brutal, and incommensurate with the number of victims on the day of 11 September. According to a report of military experts, La Moneda was hit by more than 50,000 projectiles, yet there were only two killed in the palace, Allende and Olivares, and both committed suicide. Two GAPs were injured and taken to the Central Post Office. The military lost five men killed in the centre: two sergeants, a soldier, a corporal and a carabinero. One civilian was killed; a photographer.

The second major scene of fighting was in the southern zone of Santiago. At Indumet, a carabinero was killed and two were seriously wounded, one of whom would die three days later. An MIR activist was also killed. In La Legua, six Carabineros and a socialist activist died; while a woman was fatally wounded near the Sumar plant and died two days later. Around the UTE a carabinero and a socialist activist were killed. In the rest of Santiago five workers and a housewife fell.[268]

In the provinces, a miner was killed in Vallenar, three socialists militants fell in the mountain range of Talca trying to flee the country; a carabinero was also killed during this attempt. A major and a police captain were killed by a subordinate in Antofagasta. The deaths of 11 September in the provinces, seven, were small compared to Santiago. In total, including the deaths from the actions of 11 September, 33 people were lost. This was a modest figure for the firepower deployed by the FF. AA. At the end of the day, the army took control of the country without any challenge that could call into question its authority. A new page of Chile's history opened[269].

CHAPTER 7
THE NEW REGIME

In the aftermath of 11 September, the Military Junta justified its action, before national and international public opinion, by delivering speeches on the return of law and order to Chile. But the majority, including Air General Leigh and Admiral Merino, considered Marxism not as an ideology or a method of socio-economic analysis, but as a deadly disease with an uncontrollable capacity for dissemination – as shown by the electoral progress of the UP during elections from March 1973. From that point, it was no longer a question of electoral results but of a social disease, which like a cancer, had to be eradicated by force.

From 11 September 1973, state violence swept the whole of Chile; targeting the leftist militants and leaders of the social movement. Thus began a 'dark period' for activists: times of hiding, arrests and detention, torture, death or exile. For months afterwards checkpoints were established by Carabineros and the army in all the streets of the capital, while requisitioned buses full of soldiers drove through neighbourhoods, sometimes stopping to search a home. The image of men and women pushed with rifle butts, arms over their heads, and loaded onto military trucks became familiar. By December 1973, the new regime collected more than 18,000 prisoners.[270] These were herded into hastily constructed concentration camps, usually at various sport stadiums: indeed, the National Stadium of Santiago – including a velodrome – became a symbol: thousands were detained, tortured and then murdered there, including the singer and poet Victor Jara. Hundreds of thousands of Chileans were processed by the secret service, many beaten and others tortured: thousands of them were disappeared. According to the US Ambassador to Santiago:

'Estimates of the number of people who died during or immediately after the coup vary from 2,500 to more than 80,000. A range of 3,000 to 10,000 deaths covers the most reliable estimates.'

The repression particularly hit the working class, as shown by the official statistics of the Truth and Reconciliation Committee of 1991.[271] According to political scientists like Steve J. Stern, this desire to physically eliminate as many opponents as possible could be likened to a 'politicide':

> ...a systematic project to destroy an entire way of doing and understanding politics and governance.[272]

The Caravan of Death

One of the first measures of the Junta was to crush the trade union movement and to ban the CUT. The defeat of the revolutionary movement resulted in widespread political purges in the companies, which, for the most important, ended under the military rule: there would be more than 270 detainees in the Madeco plant, 500 people immediately dismissed in the Sumar factory, while repression severely hit workers in Yarur and Cristalerias de Chile too. Many employers participated fully in the system of denunciation and arrest of activists set up by the Junta. This was precisely what happened at the Elecmetal factory, returned to its owners on 17 September. Overall, about 100,000 people were fired and black-listed by the Junta.[273]

The next phase of repression began with the creation of the National Direction for Intelligence (*Direccion de Inteligencia Nacional*, DINA), on 12 November 1973. This was little more than a body that coordinated the collection of intelligence on the Chilean population. Led by Colonel Manuel Contreras Sepúlveda, the DINA was transformed into a political police, per Pinochet's decree of 14 June 1974. Three secret articles in its statute specified that all the intelligence services of Chile were subordinate to DINA, which thus had unlimited powers to arrest – at home, if necessary, and without judicial warrants – anyone considered "suspicious."[274]

The regime of the DINA was characterised by widespread repression, massacres and countless abuses of human rights, intended to impose a climate of terror. Hundreds were disappeared: taken away from their homes and families, they were never processed through prisons or camps. Others were removed through succinct executions. Almost every day, abandoned corpses were found in other parts of Chilean cities.

The mass repression was not limited to Santiago alone. On 30 September 1973, a military convoy commanded by General Sergio Arellano left for southern Chile. The same unit was then re-deployed to the north, in mid-October. In the course of a weeks-long campaign

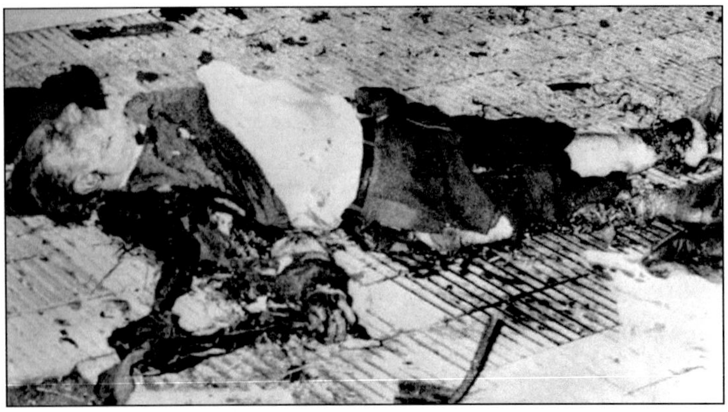

General Prats was assassinated by the DINA in Buenos Aires in September 1974. (Albert Grandolini Collection)

General Pinochet shortly after leading the coup that brought him to power. (Albert Grandolini Collection)

of terror that became known as the 'Caravan of Death', Arellano's troops were responsible for the deaths of dozens, including 15 in La Serena, 16 in Copiapo, 14 in Antofagasta, and 26 in Calama.[275]

Subsequently, the Junta moved from open repression, based on the mass executions of opponents, to a more selective and clandestine repression. DINA began acting through commandos of five or six heavily armed operatives in civilian clothes, who used to search for, and arrest, suspects wherever they found them. Blindfolded and hooded, they would be taken away in cars, without licence plates, to one of 17 secret detention centres – like Cuatro Alamos, London Nr 38 or Villa Grimaldi.[276] All were tortured, many executed and then buried illegally, their bodies thrown into the sea or the Rio Maipo, from a helicopter. Very few were released.

Gradually, the DINA began tracking not just socialist and communist activists, but also the members of the Catholic Church and PDC militants who reported numerous violations of human rights, particularly in the Vicariate of Solidarity founded by Cardinal

Pinochet with Henry Kissinger: US involvement in the coup against Allende remains a hotly-disputed topic until today. (Albert Grandolini Collection)

Santiago. Some prisoners were 'returned' to their families and jobs, to collaborate with the DINA and serve as informers. One of them was Marcia Alejandra Merino, one of MIR's leaders. Transported by car around the streets of Santiago, she was forced to denounce her comrades. A few of the 'returned' even became torturers – like Oswaldo Romo Mena, a former activists of the Socialist Popular Union.[277]

By 1974, Pinochet and his acolytes added an international dimension to their repression. In coordination with other military juntas in Latin America, and with support of the US government, they ran what became known as 'Operation Condor'. Launched in 1974, and run well into 1975 on the initiative of Colonel Contreras, this was a coordinated operation including 'security' services of Chile, Brazil, Argentina, Paraguay, Uruguay, and Bolivia, aiming to prosecute exiled leftists. The Condor netted thousands of anonymous victims – regardless if leftists, or 'just' other kinds of opposition to the governments in question: most were executed in the country where they were caught, relatively few were sent to the country of their origin. One of its victims was General Prats, who was assassinated by a bomb in Buenos Aires, in September 1974. In October 1975, Bernardo Leighton, the leader of the PDC, was shot and wounded in Rome. Orlando Letellier, former Minister of Interior and Defence in Allende's government, was murdered in Washington, in September 1976.[278]

When it became clear that the DINA was involved in the attack on Letellier, Pinochet's dictatorship was exposed to international critique. The Junta reacted by dismissing Contreras, and replacing the DINA by the National Centre of Intelligence (Centra Nacional de Intelligencia, CNI), in August 1977.[279]

While the soldiers lead the fight against Marxist subversion, General Pinochet assumed his power at the head of Chile. He was appointed "supreme leader of the nation" in June 1974, then "President of the Republic" on 17 December. At the same time, the dictatorship imposed martial law, closed the Congress, suspended the Constitution and banned all political parties – including those that supported the coup. The public administration was purged, and soldiers were placed in key positions. The freedoms of expression, publication and meeting disappeared.

The end of Allende, and UP's experience in Chile was part of a shift in global political power relations. This was a strategic victory for capitalism that allowed not only the removal of many social gains made during Allede presidency, but also to transform Chile into a real-world laboratory for a neoliberal capitalism still unknown elsewhere.

Society would be so remodelled by the 17 years of dictatorship following 11 September 1973, that they became what Tomás Moulian or Manuel Gárate called "capitalist revolution". The extent of state violence, completely disproportionate to the resistance that opposed it, could only be explained as not only a question of killing activists in the process of committing violence, but also as an act to remove the traces of the ideas of social change. In fact, massive opposition to the dictatorship was reborn only much later, in the early 1980s, during great protests.[280]

Armed Struggle against Pinochet

The MIR was hit hard by Pinochet's ruthless tactics. Among the thousands of ordinary Chilean citizens that were detained, tortured and killed were several hundred young men and women with ties to the MIR. They confessed under torture and gave away names of other members, locations of safe houses, information about attacks, etc. Although the MIR had built up a solid network of safe houses, arms dumps and information sharing during the Allende years, it was all quickly and irrevocably compromised during the first few months of the Pinochet era.

This led directly to the loss or exile of much of the MIR's leadership. In December 1973 Bautista Van Schouwen, one of the student leaders of the MIR, was detained and "disappeared." In October 1974, about a year after the coup, tortured MIR members revealed the location of a house in Santiago where Miguel Enríquez had been hiding. On 5 October, Chilean security forces stormed the house and Enríquez was killed.

On 19 February 1975, four captured MIR leaders went on national television to urge their comrades to lay down their arms. They said that the military government was interested only in reconciliation and national unity. According to the four, MIR leadership was in ruins: of the 52 members of the Central Committee, nine had been killed, 24 were in custody, ten were in exile, one had been expelled from the group, and eight were still at large. The MIR quickly issued a statement declaring the four to be traitors, but much damage had been done.

In October 1975, Chilean police were again alerted to the location of a safe house where MIR leaders were hiding out, this time in the small village of Malloco, outside of Santiago. Andres Pascal Allende, who had assumed leadership of the MIR in Chile after the death of Enríquez, was forced to flee, eventually seeing asylum at the Costa Rican Embassy.

After the loss of Enríquez, the MIR ceased to be a genuine threat to the Chilean Junta. All of its leaders were dead, captured, or in exile. Many captured MIR members were co-operating with Chilean security forces, either willingly or not. The growing reach of Operation Condor meant that nowhere was safe.[281]

Nevertheless, in September 1977 an operative known as 'Juan Miranda' arrived in Chile to put into place "Plan 78". He learnt of the precarious situation of the MIR, which now had no more than 50 members. Leaders abroad agreed on a strategy to restructure the party by reinstating politico-military cadres and launching combat actions in the country. The clandestine arrival of cadres was known as "Operation Retorno". The aim was to send exiled activists back to Chile, after training in Cuba, to rebuild MIR and to organize bases and networks of support to trigger a rural guerrilla war in the south, in the region of Nelturne in the Valdivia mountain range, which they knew well.[282]

Beginning in 1977, activists returning to Chile organized clandestine fighting groups who began small armed-actions. The first MIR bank attacks were in 1979. In April 1980, it attacked three banks in Santa Elena. In late 1979, the party leadership ordered an attack on a supermarket. After this action began the activity of the *Fuerza central* as such; the group attacked a tobacconist in Independencia and the CNI building near Irarrázaval. The operation consisted of an attack with two AK-47 rifles and two hand grenades.

Between 1979 and 1983, *Fuerza central* had armed groups and was a military force independent of other party structures. More specifically, it was a professional structure, composed mainly of cadres who had remained in Chile, supported by others who had received a high level of military preparation and who had returned illegally. Some had belonged to the Chilean armed forces until 1973. A large number of actions, perhaps the most important, had an economic purpose, as they were intended to raise funds to support the organization. At first, the organization had a combat group led by Ernesto Zúñiga Vergara who was a former member of the Navy. In the chain of command, was the Argentinian Hugo Ratier, and at the head was Arturo Villabela.[283]

The clandestine and compartmentalized conception of this military movement hampered the possibility of recruiting new cadres capable of filling the voids created by the repression. Over time, the MIR Directorate gave permission to undertake a major operation, assassinating a senior DINA official. On the morning of 15 July 1980, the group led by Ernesto Zúñiga was standing next to a pickup truck from which two men armed with AKA-47 rifles opened fire. They killed the driver and the officer of the vehicle they were targeting and the car crashed into another vehicle. The mission had been accomplished. The officer killed was Colonel Roger Vergara, Director of the Army Intelligence School. Shortly after, the *Fuerza central* attacked banks of Santa Elena. That operation was a failure that led to the death of a guerrilla.[284] In early 1981, a series of arrests removed the first combat group. It had reached its peak in 1980, when the militias led by Guillermo Rodríguez Morales, which numbered about one hundred armed men, were formed. These militias were composed of young militants with some degree of paramilitary experience but were not professionals. They were more connected to the dynamics of the mass struggle, and could act only under the conditions of street demonstrations. It was these units that protected popular protests, where small-scale paramilitary actions were carried out, such as attacks on public lighting stations, the cutting of electrical wires and the burning of vehicles.

If *Fuerza central* concentrated its actions in the cities, the MIR didn't forget its project of forming a rural guerilla. It entrusted this task to Miguel Cabrera Fernández, an activist who participated in the fight of 11 September 1973 in Nelturne. It was there that he settled, with about 20 militants, at the end of the summer of 1980. The military authorities were quickly informed of their presence and organized a vast operation involving soldiers, Carabineros and CNI agents. On 27 June 1981, army commandos invaded the guerrilla camp, from which the men managed to flee. But without food, medicine and urban support, they sent two men back to town. The two men were captured and during September and October, the remaining guerrillas were shot dead or arrested.[285] In Santiago, *Fuerza central* was also the target of CNI operations that decimated its ranks as on January 16, 1982, when Ernesto Zúñiga was shot.

Fuerza central in Santiago then split into two detachments; one of them was dismantled by the authorities in 1982, and the second had to be content to undertake minor actions. The MIR then decided to reunite the fighters in a regional military committee led by Jorge Palma Donoso. It was at this moment Chile saw widespread opposition to the military regime. Demonstrations were held in late 1982 and early 1983 as political parties began to break their lethargy and developed their activities. At this moment the military apparatus of the MIR was in a critical situation but it decided to launch a brilliant action. On 30

August 1983, a MIR commando assassinated the mayor of Santiago, General Carol Urzua Ibañez and three men of his escort. This action was condemned by the entire political opposition while the military regime increased repression.[286]

On 7 September 1983, the police surrounded a house in Santiago and stormed it. In the fight, three MIR militants were killed. A similar operation took place a few hours later near Quinta Normal. That day, MIR's military apparatus was destroyed with the death of Hugo Ratier and Arturo Villabela. The last fighters took the road of exile. The last major action of the MIR in Chile was on 26 January 1988, when the organization booby-trapped a house in La Cisterna with explosives, causing the death of the commander of the Special Operations Group of the Carabineros. With the return of democracy in 1990, the deeply divided MIR lost all political influence.

In the aftermath of the military coup, fierce debates shook the PCCh where some criticized the organisation's lack of an effective military policy before 11 September[287]. The communist leaders quickly began a revision of the political line where the armed struggle became a legitimate option against the Pinochet regime. As early as 1974, there was also the idea of having a military organization, an armed wing of the Party. But it was necessary to wait ten years before this idea was realized.

Many Chilean communists took refuge in Cuba where they received housing and employment, but where the authorities didn't repeat to them that they had to lead an armed struggle against the Pinochet regime rather than remain in exile. The Cubans didn't hesitate to accuse the Socialists and Communists of being unable to properly organize the defence of the Allende government. While the leadership of the PCCh planned to engage in armed struggle, in July 1974 Fidel Castro made an offer to Communist leaders Volodia Teitelboim and Rodrigo Rojas Castro to give military training to militants of the Young Communists; a proposal that was accepted.[288] The chosen militants then received a complete military education within the Camilo Cienfuegos Military School and became officers in the Cuban Revolutionary Armed Forces. This training lasted one year and took place both in infantry and artillery units while some specialized in the navy or aviation. Some activists were also sent to the East-Germany and Bulgaria to receive military training.[289] Graduates of the Bulgarian schools would later form the basis of the most effective guerrilla units. Thus, under the aegis of Castro, a small Chilean Red Army gradually developed.

At the end of these activities, the Cubans thought that the Chilean Communists did not yet have the capacity to face Pinochet's soldiers. Therefore, they preferred to send them to other battlefields to harden them. Many went to Nicaragua to fight alongside the Sandinistas. As such, they participated in most of the battles fought by the Sandinistas, including the seizing of Managua. After the 1979 victory, many of them stayed in Nicaragua to serve in the country's armed forces.[290]

In September 1980, the Secretary General of the PCCh, Luis Corvalán, openly declared that the use of the armed struggle was legitimate to defeat the military regime and theorized the Party line under the name of "popular mass rebellion policy". It was during the year 1983 that the PCCh organized its military apparatus which was baptized *Frente Patriotico Manuel Rodriguez* (FPMR) in honour of a hero of the fight for independence against the Spaniards. Guillermo Teillier, head of the PCCH's military commission, was responsible for overseeing the actions of this new organization. In the summer, five commanders returned to Chile to begin guerrilla warfare.[291] The supply of arms and money was provided by the Cuban intelligence services, while the nucleus of command structures in the field was entrusted to the militants who had received military training in Cuba

A group of FPMR militants in their training camp in the mid-1980s. (Albert Grandolini Collection)

and Bulgaria, or who had fought alongside Sandinistas, in other words they were experienced fighters. Among them, stood Raúl Pellegrin, second lieutenant in the Cuban Army and veteran of Nicaragua, who returned illegally to his native country in 1983 to become the main leader of the FPMR under the name of Commander José Miguel.

The first action of the FPMR in Chile took place on 14 December 1983 with the sabotage of the Curico power station, depriving the centre of the country of electricity. The actions of the FPMR were those of the urban guerrilla: bombings, sabotage, armed robberies, and the organization of kidnapping or the use of car bombs. The first operation with a national impact was the kidnapping of a journalist from the daily newspaper *La Nacion* in December 1984. FPMR took repeated actions against far-right parties and movements; targeting the printing houses of their newspapers and their buildings. The leaders of the regime were also priority targets. Thus, in 1986, Colonel Mario Aberle Rivadeneira, chief of protocol at the garrison of Santiago was kidnapped. He was released three days later without a ransom being demanded. In 1987, attacks against police patrols began, while economic targets, including US companies, were also hit.

The organization's financing and equipment supply was provided by Cuba and Eastern European countries. Thus, in May 1986, in the port of the small village of Carrizal Bajo, the men of the FPMR landed nearly 80 tons of weapons transported until then by Cuban special forces. These weapons, C-4 explosive, RPG-7 and M-72 LAW rocket launchers, and more than 3,000 M-16 assault rifles, worth $30 million, were partially of American origin from Vietnam. If the unloading of such an amount went unnoticed, many imprudent actions by activists allowed the Chilean security forces to get their hands on this impressive arsenal. By the beginning of August, nearly 90% of this material had already fallen into the hands of the authorities.[292]

The year 1986 was also the year in which the FPMR carried out an operation, under preparation since the end of 1984, under the name of Operation "20th Century" and which aimed, nothing less than, to assassinate General Pinochet. The weapons used were those landed at Carrizal Bajo and distributed before the police discovered most of the stock. The operation was conducted on the military side by Jose Valenzuela Levi, while logistics and planning were the responsibility of Cecilia Magni.

On 7 September 1986, Pinochet left his holiday home in El Melocoton to return to Santiago. The dictator's convoy was formed of five vehicles, two of which were armoured, and the heavily armed escort included both police and military. The convoy was attacked by about twenty FPMR militants armed with M-16 rifles and M-72 LAW

The Chilean Junta never let the FPMR to grow into a dangerous organisation. Nevertheless, it took care to stage propaganda operations against it too. In this case, a group of army troops acted as FPMR militants for the press. (Albert Grandolini Collection)

rocket launchers. Pinochet, who travelled in one of the two armoured vehicles, was unscathed by the attack. He owed his life to a rocket that bounced off the roof of his vehicle, rather than hitting the bodywork, and to the skill of his driver. Five of the dictator's bodyguards, however, were still killed during this operation.[293]

Despite its formal status as an armed wing of the PCCh, the FPMR was gradually becoming an autonomous organization. This situation was the result of increasing differences between the FPMR commanders, whose views were more radical, and those of PCCh's exiled leaders. The latter noted in 1987 that Pinochet still held Chile firmly, and that the military actions of the previous years hadn't changed this situation. They decided to modify their line to enable an exit of the dictatorship by political, and not only military, means.[294]

For Pellegrin, the new position taken by the PCCh meant an abandonment of military work and the marginalization of the FPMR. The rupture sealed the creation of an autonomous FPMR to which adherents trained in Cuba, like Vasili Carrilo and Galvarino Apablaza, adhered. He began publishing the newspaper *El Rodriguista* under the direction of Alex Voytovych. The conflict between the PCCh and the FPMR was nevertheless accompanied by an internal crisis within the latter. When the communist leadership called for the dissolution of the military organization, some militants obeyed and set down their arms to found the CP-Patriotic Movement Manuel Rodriguez, a group that would eventually separate from the PCCh.

In addition to this internal crisis, the repression following the attack against Pinochet weakened the FPMR. Many leaders were shot dead during Operation Albania, where 12 militants were murdered in various parts of the country, on 15 June 1987, by police and soldiers. The FPMR then embarked on a campaign targeting regime personalities such as Colonel Carlos Carreño, kidnapped in September 1987, or the attempted assassination of Prosecutor Torres in May 1988.[295] Pellegrin also engaged in what he called a "national patriotic war" in order to raise the population against Pinochet. It was during this campaign that Pellegrin died. On 21 October 1988, while trying to escape a police encirclement, FPMR fighters including Pellegrin, were arrested. His body would be found two days later in a river. The management of the FPMR then passed to Galvarino Apablaza.[296]

In spite of the break with the PCCh, Cuba continued financially supporting and assuring the armed provision of FPMR. The STASI also took an active part in helping the guerrillas. Pellegrin went to the GDR regularly, where he meet East German representatives. But funds sent from Cuba were generally deficient to finance all of the activities of the FPMR, who supplemented its needs by a policy "of dispossession" or of racketeering to collect a revolutionary tax from firms.

The end of dictatorship and return of democracy to Chile however didn't mean the end of military operations by FPMR. If the latter reduced the intensity of its actions, it continued hitting. It organised the kidnapping of the son of the owner of a big daily newspaper in September 1991. Notably, on 1 April 1991, FPMR murdered the senator Jaime Guzman. Cuba condemned this action and ceased supporting the organisation. The Chilean authorities formed an intelligence unit to fight the armed groups, particularly FPMR. In 1992, this unit, with the collaboration of former activists, arrested the authors of the kidnapping of September 1991. Badly hit by these arrests, FPMR stopped any action for a number of years. On 30 December 1996, some of these activists, in the high security prison in Santiago, managed to get away by using a helicopter. After this remarkable action, the military adventures of the FPMR ceased, and finally in 1999, it was withdrawn from the list of the terrorist organisations by the American State Department.

A last armed resistance group appeared at the beginning of 1980s. It was a period when popular demonstrations against the regime developed, demonstrations roughly suppressed by dictatorship. Within MAPU, a part of the UP which passed in hiding after September 11, deep debates took place to decide if it was necessary to struggle against the dictatorship by means of armed conflict or by means of peaceful opposition. A minority was favourable to armed conflict and, driven by Guillermo Ossandó, found the Movimiento Juvenil Lautaro. The group had lead armed actions of bomb attacks, sabotage, raids on armouries and banks, until 1988. At this point debate developed in the organisation on the choice to support peaceful transition towards democracy, or to continue armed conflict. The decision was to continue armed action, and the government of Patricio Aylwin put MAPU-MJL in the category of terrorist organizations.[297]

By a curious paradox, the military dictatorship, formed of servicemen specialising in the struggle against revolutionary war, gave rise to the conditions necessary for the development of left-wing armed groups within the political forces which had supported Allende, who at this time were opposed to violence. The American authorities were aware of this phenomenon and feared its extension. The Reagan administration tried, therefore, to promote a transition between opposition and military government while assuring the permanence of the political and economic regime established by dictatorship.

The return of Democracy

In 1980, General Pinochet adopted a new Constitution which stipulated the organisation of a referendum in 1988. If 'Yes' won, Pinochet would continue running the country for eight years longer; if it was 'No', he would have to organise elections within one year, and relinquish power. The opposition organised a broad front in favour of 'No' and formed the Concenration of Democracy (*Concertación democratica*) around the PS, PDC and the *Partido por Democracia* (PPD). In spite of the support of the press and media, the *Concertación* managed to unite about a million people in Santiago, the day before polls. On 5 October 1988, the results of referendum were unambiguous: 'No' won 54.7 % of votes.[298]

With Washington becoming anxious to get rid of a cumbersome ally at the time Cold War was about to end, the USA played a major role in this referendum. The Reagan administration supported the opposition in Chile which it financed generously, but Washington watched the military closely and sabotaged Pinochet's plans to cancel the referendum. The CIA was indeed informed that servicemen feared being pursued for crimes under the dictatorship and wanted therefore to prevent the referendum. Three days before the poll, American State Department Undersecretary, John Whitehead, officially informed Pinochet's government about Washington's concerns over a possible cancellation of the referendum.[299] The US government, that so much favoured the coup of 11 September 1973, seemingly prevented

Puchancavi concentration camp was one of the most notorious detention facilities for opponents of Pinochet's regime. (Albert Grandolini Collection)

another one on 5 October 1988. On the day of the referendum, Pinochet appeared to refuse to accept his defeat and planed to order an intervention by the High Command. However, Fernando Matthei, a member of the Junta, opposed this decision. Although a member of the High Command, he was ready to say no to Pinochet, because he knew he had the Americans in his back.[300]

The triumph of 'No' in 1988 was confirmed in March 1990 with the election, as president of the Republic, of Patricio Aylwyn, the PDC candidate. Even before Aylwin's election and inauguration, the transition pact was at work, with both sides jockeying to secure their preferred structure for the reborn democracy. The *Concertación* extracted key constitutional reforms during this period in an attempt to dilute some of the prerogatives inserted by the military for itself. Pinochet had envisioned a system of constitutionally guaranteed military tutelage following the eventual transition from his regime. The Constitution of 1980 included both direct means of military influence through a military presence in governmental institutions, as well as an indirect influence through the military's allies on the political right. Pinochet enacted laws during his final days that furthered the military's protection of its sphere. The agreement passed between the High Command and political parties regrouped within *Concertación*, was based on the affirmation of the unity of the nation, the will to maintain social stability, the cohesion of the political community, and the tacit commitment to switch attention towards the future. It was, therefore, in the name of democracy and national reconciliation, and by the virtue of a legislative device inherited from dictatorship, that the person of Pinochet avoided prosecution until the 1990s.

Pinochet not only hoped to create an influential position of power for the military within the re-democratized state, but he also sought protections that would prevent the civilian government from exercising influence over the military. One of the more notorious examples of military insulation and self-granted prerogatives remains the 1978 Amnesty Law. To protect its own against any future prosecution for the violence of its early years, the Pinochet regime passed an amnesty for acts committed between the 11 September 1973 coup and 10 March 1978. The Amnesty Law prevented prosecution for murder and torture and had remained a serious legal obstacle for human rights groups seeking justice for the military. Although the military left power quietly and without violence, it built its defences carefully before returning to the barracks. For his part, Pinochet did not step very far from the limelight: he remained in control of the High Command for another eight years, seated in the Ministry of Defence, from where he had a nice view of La Moneda. Pinochet remained C-in-C until 1998 when he left this function to become a lifelong senator. The immunity which this post gave him continued sheltering him from prosecution.

Memory and Juridical Struggle

With the return of democracy, the victims of the dictatorship and their fellows asked that justice was made for crimes made since 11 September 1973. One of the first political acts of Patricio Aylwyn was to constitute a National Committee of the Truth and of Reconciliation, by a decree of 25 April 1990. In February 1991, this committee published a report (known as the Rettig Report) that drew a nominal balance of repression – from 2,922 to 3,197 people killed or disappeared. Proclaimed 'the official truth', this figure served as a basis for the politics of reparations made to the victims.[301] While supposed to appease tensions within Chilean society and to anchor everybody in a new democratic epoch, it became symbolic for its incomplete character and as an attempt to cover up the issue of the violation of human rights in the public debate.

In the early 1990s, organisations of victims' families, like *Agrupación of Familiares de los Detenidos Desaparecidos* (founded in 1975 to collect information on political suppression) and *Corporación of Promoción y Defensa de los Derechos del Pueblo* (founded in November 1980), further intensified denunciation of the violations of human rights by Pinochet's regime. Their activity resulted in several trials. However, Pinochet was never directly accused, and those culpable for the crimes in question were protected by the Amnesty Law of 1978.[302] Pinochet was further protected through immunity conferred by his position as a life-long senator. Thus, and at most, those indicted of crimes against humanity were his henchmen – like General Contreras, former chief of the DINA, who was sentenced in 1993, to seven years in prison for Letellier's assassination. Even this judgement became possible only because Letellier had been killed in Washington, and together with his secretary, who was a US citizen.[303] Although the *Concertación* government tried to show this act as a proof that the rule of law and order was restored, Chilean democracy remained no less marked with the stamp of impotence.

It was thus only Pinochet's arrest in London, in October 1998, that finally marked a decisive break: for the first time, a former leader of the state was charged for 'torture, terrorism, and genocide'. [304] While this arrest caused a month-long 'battle' between medical experts, Pinochet was finally sent back to Chile – only to receive a triumphant welcome from representatives of former Frei government and the High Command of the Chilean Armed Forces. For a few days, it appeared his case would never be closed. However, the atmosphere in the country had changed meanwhile – so also within the judicial domain. In May 2000, Pinochet's immunity was lifted, and in December of the same year he was indicted for 'intellectual responsibility' in the case of 18 disappearances and 57 homicides in the course of the Caravan of Death.[305]

Leaning on nearly 300 legal proceedings in Europe, and supported by the socialist government elected in 1999, the subsequent juridical process de-facto ended the period of immunity for all the members of the armed forces. Although the Supreme Court dismissed Pinochet's indictment for medical reasons in July 2002, he was forced to resign from his senatorial seat shortly after, and charged for several crimes – including the assassination of General Prats and the murder of 119 in Operation Colombo – in December 2004. In January 2005, the Chilean Army accepted institutional responsibility for past human rights abuses.[306] A year later, Pinochet was indicted for kidnappings and torture at the Villa Grimaldi detention centre by judge Alejandro Madrid. On 25 November 2006, Pinochet marked his 91st birthday by having his wife read a statement he had written to admirers present for his birthday:

> I assume the political responsibility for all that has been done.[307]

Two days later, he was sentenced to house arrest for the kidnapping and murder of two bodyguards of Salvador Allende who were arrested the day of the 1973 coup, and executed by firing squad during the 'Caravan of Death'.[308] Pinochet died on 10 December 2006, without having been convicted of any of the crimes of which he was accused.

Memory of 11 September 1973 and the military dictatorship is far from being appeased in Chile. While the town council of Providencia decided to change the name of an avenue to 11 September, in 2013, there are still hundreds of streets, places and avenues in other Chilean cities paying a tribute to the coup.[309] According to the report introduced by the programme of the human rights of the Home Office, 1,372 agents of the dictatorship were revealed, accused and condemned by 2015. Among these, only 163 were sentenced to prison, of which only 117 were still in prison. While the number of victims of the dictatorship exceeds 40,000, most their persecutors benefited from the Amnesty Law of 1978.[310]

Every September in Chile thus remains a trip into the country's history. There are numerous commemoration services during the week before the 11th, and the month is generally filled with important announcements. In 2017, Michelle Bachelet, the president of the country, in her homage to Salvador Allende announced her decision to publish all the remaining secret documents via the Valech Committee. Created in 2003, and including acknowledged experts, the latter is listing the crimes committed during the dictatorship – the list of which has remained secret over nearly 50 years. On 11 September 2017, 4,000 people went onto the streets of Santiago to remember 11 September 1973, while the University of Chile issued posthumous certificates to 104 students killed or disappeared under dictatorship.[311] Judicial proceedings are still going on: the battle for Chile is still not over.

SELECTED BIBLIOGRAPHY

Agüero, Felipe, 'Militares, Estado y Sociedad en Chile: Mirando el Futuro Desde la Comparación Histórica', (*Revista de cienca politica*, Vol XXII, n° 1, 2002)

Amorós, Mario, *Allende: La biografía,* (Barcelona: Grupo Zeta, 2013), ISBN 978-84-666-5378-7

Andrés Sujatt, Julio, 'La Junta de Coodinación Revolucionaria (1972-1979). Une experiencia de internacionalismo armado en el Cono Sur de América Latina', https://dialnet.unirioja.es/descarga/articulo/6114364.pdf

Arancibia C., Patricia, Balart Páez, Francisco, Brahm García, Enrique, San Francisco, Alejandro *El ejército de los chilenos 1540-1920,* (Biblioteca Americana, 2007), ISBN 978-956-8239-19-0

Bitar, Sergio, *Chile 1970-1973: asumir la historia para construir el futuro,* (Pehuen Editores, 1996), ISBN 956-160288-1

Blasco Rovira, Anne M. & Sierpe, Vladimir, 'Militantismo y resistancia socialista chilena entre 1973 y 1975: historia de un sacrificio' (*Revista de Historia Social y de los Mentalidades*, Vol . 19, n°1, 2015)

Castillo, Carmen, *Un jour d'octobre à Santiago,* (éditions Stock, 1980), ISBN 978-2736000707

Cavallo, Ascanio, Sepúlveda, Oscar, Salazar Manuel, *La historia occulta del regimen militar: Chile 1973-1988,* (Grupo Grijalbo-Mondadori, 2001), ISBN 956-258-112-8

Cavallo, Ascanio & Serrano Margarita, *Golpe 11 de septiembre de 1973: Las 24 horas más dramáticas del siglo XX,* (Uqbor Editorec, 2013), ISBN 978-956-9171-24-6

Chasteen, John Charles, *Born in Blood and Fire: A Concise History of Latin America,* (W.W Norton and Company, 2001), ISBN 978-0393976137

Collier Simon & Sater, William F. *History of Chile, 1808-1994,* (Cambridge University Press, 1996), ISBN 0-521-56075-6

Comisión nacional de verdad y reconciliación, Informe, (Secretaría de Comunicación y Cultura, 1991): http://bibliotecadigital.indh.cl/handle/123456789/170

Constable, Pamela & Valenzuelo Arturo, *A nation of enemies. Chile under Pinochet,* (W.W. Norton & Company, 1993), ISBN 978-0393309850

Debray, Régis, *Entretien avec Allende sur la situation au Chili,* (Points-Seuil, 1974)

Dinges, John, *Les années Condor,* (La Découverte, 2004), ISBN 2-7071-4424-X

Edwards, Sebastian & Edwards Alejandra C., 'The Chilean experiment: an Overview', (Working Paper Number 397, University of California, 1986)

El Semanal-La Tercera, "Especial, Los 22 días que sacudieron a Chile", (n° 119, September 2013)

Ensalaco, Mark, *Chile under Pinochet: Recovering the truth,* (University of Pennsylvania Press, 2000), ISBN 0-8122-3520-7

Fernández Camilo & Garrido Pablo, 'Progresistas y revolucionarios: el Frente de Acción Popular y la vía chilena al socialismo, 1956- 1967', *Izquierdas*, n° 31, december 2016

Fontaine Talavera, Arturo, 'The United States and the Soviet Union in Chile', (Estudios Publicos, 72, Spring 1998)

Garcés, Joan, *Allende y la experiencia chilena. Las armas de la política,* (Bat, 1990), ISBN 978-8432316487

Garcés Joan, *Soberanos e intervenidos. Chile la Guerra Fría y después,* (Ed. BAT, 1995), ISBN 956-70-2226-7

Garcés, Marío & Leiva, Sebastián, *El Golpe en la Legua Los caminos de la historia y de la memoria,* (Lom Historia, 2005), ISBN 956-282712-7

García, Pio, *Las Fuerzas Armardas y el golpe de Estado en Chile,* (Siglo Veintuno, 1974)

Gaudichaud, Franck, *Chili 1970-1973: Mille jours qui ébranlèrent le monde,* (Presses Universitaires de Rennes, 2013), ISBN 978-2-7535-2663-1

Goicovic Donoso, Igor & Lisboa Freire, Evandro, 'The development of the popular movement and rise of the revolutionary left in Chile (1953-1978)', (*Tempo e Argumento,* Vol 7, n° 16, 2015)

González, Ignacio, *El día en que murió Allende,* (Cesoc, 1990), ISBN 9789563241969

González, Monica, *La conjura,: los mil y un días de un golpe,* (Ediciones B, 2000), ISBN 956-751054-7

Guardiola-Rivera, Oscar, *Story of Death Foretold: The Coup against Salvador Allende,* (Bloomsbury, 2013), ISBN 978-1-408-85476-1

Harmer, Tanya, *The Rules of the Game: Allende's Chile, The United States and Cuba. 1970-1973,* (Thesis, London School of Economics, 2008)

Harvey, Robert, *Liberators: Latin America's Struggle for Independence*, (The Overlook Press, 2000), ISBN 978-1585670727

Joxe, Alain, *Las Fuerzas Armadas en el Sistema Político de Chile*, (Editorial Universitaria, 1970)

Kalfon, Pierre, *Allende. Chili: 1970-1973*, (Atlantica, 2000), ISBN 978-2843940903

Kornbluh, Peter, *The Pinochet File: A Declassified Dossier on Atrocity and Accountability*, (The new Press, 2013), ISBN 978-1595589125

Larrain, Sergio, *The Chilean Army, its history, organization, regional environment and challenges over the next 25 years*, (US Army War College, 2002)

Lefranc, Sandrine, *Politiques du pardon*, (Presses Universitaires de France, 2002), ISBN 2-13-052401-X

López Tobar, Mario, *El 11 en la mira de un Hawker Hunter. Las operaciones y blancos aéreos de septiembre de 1973*, (Santiago: Sudamericana, 1999), ISBN 978-9562620864

Nolff, Max, *Salvador Allende: El político: El estadista*, (Ediciones Documentas, 1993), ISBN 983.064 092

Magasich, Jorge, *Los que dijeron 'No'. Historia del movimiento de los marinos antigolpistas de 1973*, (Ed. LOM, 2008), ISBN 978-956-282968-7

Mitrokhin, Vasili & Andrew, Christopher, *The World Was Going Our Way: The KGB and the Battle for the Third World*, (Basic Books, 2005), ISBN 978-0-465-00311-2

Moyano Barahona, Cristina, *El MAPU durante la dictatura*, (Ediciones, Universitad Alberto Hurtado, 2010), ISBN 9789-5-693-2031-6

Patino, Bruno, *Pinochet s'en va… La transition démocratique au Chili (1988-1994)*, (IHEAL, 2000), ISBN 2-907163-79-5

Peña, Juan Cristóbal, *Los fusileros: Cronica secreta de un guerilla en Chile*, (Penguin Ramdom House, 2016), ISBN 9789569545290

Pérez, Cristián, 'Salvador Allende, apuntes sobre su dispositivo de seguridad: El grupo de amigos personales (GAP)', (*Estudios Publicos*, 79, Winter 2000)

Pérez, Cristián, 'Historia del Mir', (*Estudios Publicos*, Winter 2003)

Pérez, Cristián, 'Che Guevara's Army and its Chilean followers', (*Estudios Publicos*, 89, Summer 2003)

Pérez, Cristián, 'Años de disparos y tortura (1973-1975): Los ultímos dias de Miquel Enríquez', (*Estudios Publicos*, Spring 2004)

Pérez Carillo, David, *La fronda militar: el 11 de septiembre*, (Magíster en Ciencia Política, Universidad de Chile, Instituto, september 2006)

Pérez Silva, Claudio, 'El Frente Antifascista y la Politica Militar del Partido Comunista de Chile bajo dictatura, 1973-1980', (*Tempo e Argumento*, vol. 7, n° 16, september-december 2015)

Politzer, Patricia, *Altamirano*, (Ediciones Melquíades, 1989), ISBN 978-9506990206

Prats, Carlos, *Memorias: testimonio de un soldado*, (Editorial Pehuen, 1985), ISBN 978-9561601291

Quiroga, Patricio, *Compañeros. El GAP: la escolta de Allende*, (Aguilar, 2001), ISBN 978-9562391870

Reeves, Richard, *President Nixon: Alone in the White House*, (Simon and Schuster, 2002), ISBN 0-684-80231-7

Robin, Marie-Monique, *Escadrons de la mort, l'école française*, (La Découverte, 2004), ISBN 2-7071-4163-1

Rojas, Robinson, *Estos mataron a Allende*, (Martinez Roca, 1974), ISBN 84-270-0266-1

San Francisco, Alejandro & Soto, Ángel (éd.), *Camino a La Moneda, Las elecciones presidenciales en la historia de Chile 1920-2000*, (Editorial Antártica, 2005), ISBN 956-8147-22-5

Sarget, Marie-Nöelle, *Histoire du Chili de la conquête à nos jours*, (L'Harmattan, 1996), ISBN 2-7384-4593-4

Sigmund, Paul E., *The overthrow of Allende and the politics of Chile, 1964-1976*, (University of Pittsburgh Press, 1977), ISBN 0-8229-3355-1

Soto, Oscar, *El último día de Salvador Allende*, (Aguilar, 1998), ISBN 978-8403593879

Stern, Steve J., *Remembering Pinochet's Chile: On the Eve of London 1998*, (Duke University Press, 2009) ISBN 0-8223-3354-6

Torrejón-Barreda, Carolina, 'La clandestinité rêvée, la clandestinité subie. Parcours clandestins du Parti socialiste du Chili, 1959-1979', (*Bulletin de l'Institut Pierre Renouvin*, 2013/2)

Vega, Luis, *La Caída de Allende: anatomía de un golpe de estado*, (La Semana Publicaciones, 1983), ISBN 978-9568421434

Veneros, Diana, *Allende: Un ensayo psicobiográfico* (Señales, 2003), ISBN 956-262181-2

Verdugo, Patricia, *Interferencia secreta. 11 de septiembre de 1973*, (Sudamericana, 1998), ISBN 978-9563244519

Verdugo, Patricia, *Operación siglo XX. El atentado a Pinochet*, (Editorial Catalonia, 2016) ISBN 978-9563244014

Whelan, James, *Allende: Death of a marxist dream*, (Westport: Arlington House, 1981), ISBN 978-0870005039

Witker, Alejandro, *Salvador Allende, 1908–1973. Prócer de la liberación nacional*, (National Autonomous University of Mexico, 1980), ISBN 968-58-2754-0

Zamora, Sergio, *Histoire d'une trahison: 11 septembre 1973, coup d'Etat au Chili*, (Yvelinedition, 2013), ISBN 978-2-84668-454-5

Much information can be consulted on various websites and online archives like nsa.org, cia.org, memoriachilena.cl, gobiernodechile.cl, fundacionsalvadorallende.cl.

Many fiction or documentary films concerned the 11 September 1971 coup, the most famous fiction movie, *Missing*, was directed by Costa-Gavras in 1982, and the best documentary film is *Battle of Chile* by Patricio Guzman.

NOTES

1 Marie-Noelle Sarget, *Histoire du Chili de la conquête à nos jours*, L'Harmattan, 1996, pp. 12-13.

2 Ibid, pp. 26-27.

3 Ibid, pp. 38-40 and Robert Harvey, *Liberators: Latin America's Struggle for Independence*, New York, The Overlook Press, 2000

4 Marie-Noelle Sarget, op.cit. p. 51.

5 Ibid, pp. 65-66.

6 Ibid, p. 115.
7 Ibid, pp. 86-93.
8 Ibid, pp. 131-132.
9 Ibid, p. 144. The former League of Nations declared Chile for the 'most affected nation' of that crisis.
10 Ibid, p. 158.
11 Ibid, p. 165.
12 Ibid, p. 178.
13 Ibid, p. 179.
14 Camilo Fernández y Pablo Garrido. 'Progresistas y revolucionarios: el Frente de Acción Popular y la vía chilena al socialismo, 1956- 1967' *Izquierdas*, n° 31, december 2016, pp. 71-101 & Marie-Noëlle Sarget, p. 203.
15 Debray, *Entretien avec Allende sur la situation au Chili*, Points-Seuil, 1974, p. 72-73.
16 Diana Veneros, *Allende: Un ensayo psicobiográfico* (Santiago, Chile: Señales, 2003), p. 38.
17 Ibid, p. 44.
18 Regis Debray, p. 70.
19 Alejandro Witker, *Salvador Allende, 1908–1973. Prócer de la liberación nacional* , National Autonomous University of Mexico, 1980), pp. 4–5.
20 Régis Debray, p. 73.
21 Max Nolff, *Salvador Allende: El político: El estadista* (Ediciones Documentas, 1993), 32.
22 San Francisco, Alejandro & Soto, Ángel, *Las elecciones presidenciales en la historia de Chile 1920-2000*, (Editorial Antártica, 2005), p. 272.
23 Régis Debray, p. 79.
24 San Francisco, Alejandro & Soto, Ángel, p. 331.
25 Marie-Noëlle Sarget, p. 212.
26 Marie-Noëlle Sarget, p. 215; Vasili Mitrokhin & Christopher Andrew. *The World Was Going Our Way: The KGB and the Battle for the Third World*, (Basic Books, 2005), pp. 69-88.
27 Chileanization of copper, was a progressive process by which the Chilean government acquired control of the major foreign-owned section of the Chilean copper mining industry.
28 Ibid, p. 220.
29 Tanya Harmer, *The Rules of the Game: Allende's Chile, The United States and Cuba. 1970-1973*, (Thesis, London School of Economics, 200),8 p. 48. According to Harmer, Frei received no less than US$3 million in financial support from Washington.
30 Richard Reeves, *President Nixon: Alone in the White House*,(Simon and Schuster, 2002), p. 259
31 Tanya Harmer, p. 47
32 Mario Amorós, *Allende: La biografía* (Grupo Zeta, 2013), pp. 284-285.
33 Tanya Harmer, p. 48.
34 Richard Reeves, p. 259.
35 John Dinges, *Les années Condor*, (La découverte, 2004), p. 32.
36 The "Schneider Doctrine" was espoused by General Schneider at the time of the 1970 presidential election. Schneider expressed the apolitical role of the military and his opposition to preventing Allende's presidency by a coup d'état.
37 Marie Nöelle Sarget, p. 220.
38 Tanya Harmer, p. 56
39 Salvador Allende, 'Victory Speech to the People of Santiago' (Marxists.org)
40 Régis Debray, pp. 92-98
41 Alberto Martínez, "Economía y correlación de fuerzas sociales en la transición: El caso de Chile en el período 1970–73," in (ed). Lawner, Soto, and Schatan, *Salvador Allende, Presencia en la ausencia*, (LOM Cenda, 2008), pp. 111–113.
42 Marie-Noëlle Sarget, p. 217.
43 Sebastian Edwards, Alejandra C. Edwards, *The Chilean experiment: an Overview*, University of California, 1986, p. 10.
44 Ibid, p. 11.
45 Franck Gaudichaud, *Chili 1970-1973: Mille jours qui ébranlèrent le monde*, (Presses Universitaires de Rennes, 2013), p. 75.
46 Margaret Power, *Right-wing women in Chile, Feminine Power and the Struggle against Allende, 1964-1973*, (The Pennsylvania University Press, 2002)
47 Franck Gaudichaud, p. 71.
48 Tanya Harmer, p. 107.
49 Mark Ensalaco, *Chile under Pinochet: Recovering the truth*, (University of Pennsylvania Press, 2000) p. 6.
50 Simon Collier& William F. Sater, p 343.
51 Simon Collier & William F. Sater, p 351.
52 'El poder popular: Cordónes y comandos', (*El Semanal-La Tercera*, n° 119, September 2013), pp. 31-32.
53 Ibid, p. 32.
54 Tanya Harmer, p. 176.
55 Ibid, p. 135.
56 Sergio Bitar, Chile *1970-1973: asumir la historia para construir el futuro*, (Pehuen Editores, 1996), pp. 172-174.
57 'Los Gremios: La guerra como une paro', (*El Semanal-La Tercera*, n° 119, September 2013), pp. 18-19.
58 Sergio Bitar, p. 181.
59 Trumper, Camilo D, 'The Día del Silencio and the Everyday as Political», *"A Ganar la Calle:" The Politics of Public Space and Public Art in Santiago Chile, 1970-1973* (PhD of philosophy in history, University of California, 2011) p. 181.
60 Marie-Noëlle Sargent, p. 230.
61 'Economía: Tres días de harina', (*El Semanal-La Tercera*, n° 119, September 2013), pp. 32-33.
62 Simon Collier & William F. Sater, pp 354-355.
63 Sergio Bitar, pp. 242-245
64 Arancibia C., Patricia; Balart Páez, Francisco; Brahm García, Enrique; San Francisco, Alejandro (Biblioteca Americana, 2007). El ejército de los chilenos 1540-1920, p 31.
65 Ibid, pp 58-59.
66 Ibid, pp. 83-91.
67 Georg von Rauch, *Conflict in the Southern Cone*. (Praeger publishers, 1999)
68 Arancibia C., Patricia; Balart Páez, Francisco; Brahm García, Enrique; San Francisco, Alejandro, pp. 127-131.
69 Alain Joxe, *Las Fuerzas Armadas en el Sistema Político de Chile*. (Editorial Universitaria, 1970), pp. 48-51.
70 Sergio Larrain, *The Chilean Army, its history, organization, regional environnment and challenges over the next 25 years*, (US Army War College, 2002), p. 2
71 David Pérez Carillo, *La fronda militar: el 11 de septiembre*, (Magíster en Ciencia Política, Universidad de Chile, Instituto, september 2006), pp. 17-20.
72 Robinson Rojas, *Estos mataron a Allende*, (Martinez Roca, 1974), p. 17-18 & Gazmuri Christian, 'Las armas chilenas 1975-1982', (*Defensa y Desarme America Latina y el Caribe*, vol 1, n° 1, september-december 1985), p 1-2.
73 Ibid, p. 2.
74 Robinson Rojas, p. 19.
75 Felipe Agüero, 'Militares, Estado y Sociedad en Chile: Mirando el Futuro Desde la Comparación Histórica', (*Revista de cienca politica*, Vol XXII, n° 1, 2002),
76 Alain Joxe, pp. 50-51
77 Felipe Agüero, p. 45
78 Ibid, p. 46.
79 Garcés Joan, 1995, *Soberanos e intervenidos. Chile la Guerra Fría y después*, (Ed. BAT, 1995), p. 59.
80 Ibid, pp. 34-35
81 Alain Joxe, pp. 95-97
82 Magasich Jorge, *Los que dijeron 'No'. Historia del movimiento de los marinos antigolpistas de 1973*, (Ed. LOM. 2008, Vol 1), 188-197.
83 Felipe Agüero, p. 47
84 Ibid, pp. 47-48
85 Green & Fricker, *The Air Forces of the World*, p66
86 Inigo Guevara y Moyano, *Latin American Fighters* (Houston, Harpia Publishing, 2009; ISBN: 978-0-0925539-0-9), p75
87 Ibid & Dan Hagedorn & Leif Hellström, *Foreign Invaders* (1994, Midland Publishing Ltd., ISBN: 1-85780-013-3)
88 Green & Fricker, *The Air Forces of the World*, p67
89 W. A. Harrison, *de Havilland Vampire* (Warpaint Series No.27), (Hall Park Books Ltd., ISSN 1363-0369)
90 Barry Jones, *Hawker Hunter* (1998, The Crowood Press Ltd, ISBN 1-86126-083-0) & Allan W Hall, *Hawker Hunter* (Warpaint Series No. 8), (Hall Park Books Ltd., ISSN 1363-0369). Six ex-RAF FGA.Mk 9s were added at a later date.
91 Ibid, p 2.
92 Mario Amorós, p. 252.
93 Pio Garcia, *Las Fuerzas Armardas y el golpe de Estado en Chile*, (Siglo Veintuno, 1974), p. XVII.
94 Luis Vega, *La Caída de Allende: anatomía de une golpe de estado*, (La Semana Publicaciones, 1983), p. 128 & Salvador Allende, *su pensamiento político*, (Granica Editor, 1973), p.153
95 Alain Joxe, pp. 84-97.

96 Franck Gaudichaud, p. 272.
97 On the ELN see Cristián Pérez, 'Che Guevara's Army and its Chilean followers', (*Estudios Publicos*, 89, summer 2003)
98 Carolina Torrejón-Barreda, 'La clandestinité rêvée, la clandestinité subie. Parcours clandestins du Parti socialiste du Chili, 1959-1979', (*Bulletin de l'Institut Pierre Renouvin*, 2013/2), pp. 109-122.
99 Anne M. Blasco Rovira & Vladimir Sierpe, 'Militantismo y resistancia socialiste chilena entre 1973 y 1975: historia de une sacrificio', (*Revista de Historia Social y de los Mentalidades*, Vol . 19, n°1, 2015), p.114.
100 Ascanio Cavallo, *Golpe 11 de septiembre de 1973.: Las 24 horas más dramáticas del siglo XX*, (Uqbor Editorec, Santiago, 2013), p. 64.
101 Cristián Pérez, 'Salvador Allende, apuntes sobre su dispositivo de seguridad: El grupo des amigos personales (GAP)', (*Estudios Publicos*, 79, Winter 2000), p. 50. It is known that a large group of PS' activists was still undergoing training in Cuba at the time of the coup of 11 September 1973.
102 Patricio Quiroga, *Compañeros. El GAP: la escolta de Allende*, (Aguilar, 2001), pp 83-84.
103 Ascanio Cavallo, p. 64.
104 Cristián Pérez, 'La metamorfosis del ELN chileno. Une caso de realismo politico' (eltallerchile.wordpress.com)
105 Franck Gaudichaud, p. 273.
106 Igor Goicovic Donoso & Evandro Lisboa Freire, 'The development of the popular movement and rise of the revolutionary left in Chile (1953-1978)', (*Tempo e Argumento*, Vol.7, n° 16), pp. 329-352.
107 Franck Gaudichaud, p. 50.
108 Igor Goicovic Donoso & Evandro Lisboa Freire, p. 340.
109 Franck Gaudichaud, p. 273.
110 Ibid, p. 273.
111 Ibid, p. 275.
112 Cristián Pérez, 'Salvador Allende, apuntes sobre su dispositivo de seguridad', pp40
113 Ibid, p45 & Ascanio Cavallo, p. 57
114 Cristián Pérez, 'Salvador Allende, apuntes sobre su dispositivo de seguridad', p. 48 & Ascanio Cavallo, pp57-61
115 Cristián Pérez, 'Salvador Allende, apuntes sobre su dispositivo de seguridad)', p. 48 & Ascanio Cavallo, p. 49. Contrary to what some of the US media subsequently reported, the listed firearms represented the largest supply of Cuban-sources arms to the Chilean leftists during this period. Even then, a significant portion of armament was actually handed over to the military wing of the PS.
116 Ibid, pp 53-54
117 Ibid, p56
118 Arturo Fontaine Talavera, 'The United States and the Soviet Union in Chile', (*Estudios Publicos*, 72, Spring 1998), p. 7
119 Franck Gaudichaud, p. 272
120 Oscar Guardiola-Rivera, *Story of Death Foretold: The Coup against Salvador Allende*, (Bloomsbury, 2013), p. 194.
121 Jacob Jose, 'The Case of Charles Horman Revisited: Complication and Conflict within Declassification' (College of Willian and Mary, W&M Publish, 5-2015), p. 23
122 Ibid, p 196.
123 Ascanio Cavallo, p. 259.
124 'Patria y Libertad, Alma de sabotage', (*El Semanal-La Tercera*, n° 119, September 2013), pp. 14-15
125 Jorge Magasich, Vol 2, p. 17.
126 Ascanio Cavallo, p. 28
127 Ibid, p. 28.
128 Ibid, p. 29; Eugenia Ahumada et al, Chile: la memoria prohibida I, (Pehuén Editores, 1989), p. 17 & Carlos Prats, *Memorias: testimonio de un soldado*, (Editorial Pehuen, 1985), pp. 418-419
129 Carlos Prats, p. 419.
130 Ibid, p 420.
131 Eugenio Ahumada, p. 18.
132 Carlos Prats, p. 420.
133 Ibid, p. 421.
134 'Patria y Libertad, Alma de sabotage', (*El Semanal-La Tercera*, n° 119, September 2013), pp. 14-15.
135 Ascanio Cavallo, p. 29.
136 .
137 Pio Garcia, p. XXXIX.
138 'Patria y Libertad, Alma de sabotage', (*El Semanal-La Tercera*, n° 119, September 2013), pp. 14-15.
139 Tanya Harmer, p. 177.
140 Paul E. Sigmund,, *The overthrow of Allende and the politics of Chile, 1964-1976*, (Pittsburgh: University of Pittsburgh Press, 1977), pp. 237.
141 Ascanio Cavallo, p. 31.
142 Monica Gonález, pp. 245-248
143 Ascanio Cavallo, p. 36.
144 Ibid, p. 24.
145 Ibid, p 32.
146 José Magasich, *Los que dijeron ¡No! Historia del movimiento de los marinos antigolpistas de 1973*, (LOM Ediciones, 2008)
147 Ascanio Cavallo, p. 39.
148 Tanya Harmer, pp. 173-174.
149 Joan Garcés, *Allende y la experiencia chilena. Las armas de la política*, (Bat, 1990), p. 365.
150 Ascanio Cavallo, pp. 44-46 and 'Carabineros: la tactica Yovane', (*El Semanal-La Tercera*, n° 119, September 2013), p. 28.
151 Ascanio Cavallo, p. 75.
152 'El plebiscito: La ultima hoguera', (*El Semanal-La Tercera*, n° 119, September 2013), p.39.
153 Tanya Harmer, p. 181.
154 Ibid, p. 180.
155 Joan Garcés,: *Allende y la experiencia chilena*, p. 317-318.
156 Mario López Tobar, *El 11 en la mira de un Hawker Hunter. Las operaciones y blancos aéreos de septiembre de 1973*, (Sudamericana, 1999), pp. 88-91.
157 Tanya Harmer, p. 167
158 John Dinges *Les années Condor*, (La Découverte, 2004), p 58.
159 https://www.cia.gov/library/reports/general-reports-1/chile/
160 Tanya Harmer, pp. 170-171.
161 Ibid, p. 173 & 'Brasil: A conexão secreta', (*El Semanal-La Tercera*, n° 119, September 2013), pp.24-25
162 Tanya Harmer p. 182.
163 Ibid, p. 176.
164 Ibid, p. 176.
165 Ibid, p. 176.
166 Ascanio Cavallo, p. 79.
167 David Pérez Carrillo, p 152.
168 Ascanio Cavallo, p. 79.
169 David Pérez Carrillo, p. 147
170 Ascanio Cavallo, p. 79.
171 Ascanio Cavallo, p. 78.
172 David Pérez, pp. 149-151.
173 David Pérez Carrillo, pp. 151-152.
174 Asçanio Cavallo, pp. 125-126.
175 David Pérez Carrillo, pp. 153-154.
176 Ascanio Cavallo, p. 126
177 David Pérez Carrillo, pp. 155-157.
178 Cristian Pérez, 'Historia del MIR', (*Estudios Publicos*, Winter 2003), p. 25.
179 Ascanio Cavallo, pp. 125-127.
180 David Pérez Carrillo, p. 150.
181 Ascanio Cavallo, p. 93.
182 Patricia Verdugo, *Interferencia secreta. 11 de septiembre de 1973*, (Sudamericana, 1998), p. 50.
183 Mario Tobar López, pp. 103-118.
184 Christian Perez,'Salvador Allende, apuntes sobre su dispositivo de seguridad)', p. 36.
185 Ascanio Cavallo, p. 133.
186 Ibid, p. 99.
187 Pierre Kalfon, *Allende. Chili: 1970-1973*, (Atlantica, 2000), pp. 253-254.
188 Ascanio Cavallo, p. 102.
189 Ibid, p. 101.
190 Ibid, p. 104.
191 Ibid, p. 113.
192 Ibid, p. 96.
193 Oscar Guardiola-Rivera, p. 287.
194 Ascanio Cavallo, p. 115.
195 Cristian Perez,'Salvador Allende, apuntes sobre su dispositivo de seguridad)', p. 69.
196 Tanya Harmer, p. 185.
197 'Las 24 horas más dramáticas del siglo', "La Época, 1993", p. 7.
198 Ascanio Cavallo, p. 128.
199 Mario Tobar López, pp. 118-119.
200 Tanya Harmer, p. 185.
201 Ascanio Cavallo p. 129.
202 Patricia Verdugo, p. 74-76.

203 Patricio Quiroga, pp 180-181.
204 Hugh O'Shaughnessy, 'Chilean Coup: 40 Years ago I watched Pinochet crush a Democratic Dream', *The Guardian*, 7 September 2013
205 Ascanio Carvallo, p. 136.
206 https://www.marxists.org/archive/allende/1973/september/11.htm
207 Ascanio Cavallo, p. 143.
208 Oscar Guardiola-Rivera, p. 313.
209 Ascanio Cavallo, p. 148.
210 Tanya Harmer, p. 186.
211 Mario Tobar López, pp. 128-129.
212 Ascanio Cavallo, p. 165.
213 Ibid, p. 168.
214 Monica González, pp. 337-338.
215 Patricio Quiroga, pp. 155-161.
216 Ascanio Cavallo, p. 165.
217 Monica González, p. 362.
218 Ascanio Cavallo, p. 169.
219 Patricia Verdugo, p. 150-52.
220 Ibid, p. 137-143.
221 Ascanio Cavallo, pp. 180-181.
222 Oscar Guardiola-Rivera, p. 313.
223 Oscar Soto, *El último día de Salvador Allende*, (Aguilar, 1998), pp. 92-94.
224 Ascanio Cavallo, p. 187.
225 James Whelan, *Allende: Death of a marxist dream*, (Arlington House, 1981), pp. 201-204.
226 Ascanio Cavallo, p. 193.
227 Ibid, p. 202.
228 Ibid, p. 207-208.
229 Ibid, p. 248.
230 Comisión nacional de verdad y reconciliación, *Informe final*, (Secretaría de Comunicación y Cultura, 1991).
231 Patricia Politzer, *Altamirano*, (Ediciones B-Melquíades, 1989), pp. 28-29.
232 Luz Arce, *El infierno*, (Planeta, 1993), pp. 37-40.
233 Ascanio Cavallo, p. 135.
234 Patricia Politzer, pp. 47-49.
235 Ascanio Cavallo, p. 106.
236 Ibid, p. 132.
237 Franck Gaudichaud, p. 286.
238 Tanya Harmer, p. 187.
239 Ascanio Cavallo, p. 172.
240 Carmen Castillo, *Un jour d'octobre à Santiago*, (Éditions Stock, 1980), pp. 24-26.
241 Oscar Guardiola-Rivera, p. 330.
242 Ascanio Cavallo, p. 234.
243 Ascanio Cavallo, p. 234.
244 Oscar Guardiola-Rivera, p. 330.
245 The following account of the fighting in La Legua is largely based on Marío Garcés & Sebastián Leiva, *El Golpe en la Legua Los caminos de la historia y de la memoria*, (Lom Historia, 2005) et Ascanio Cavallo, *Golpe 11 de septiembre de 1973*.
246 Ascanio Cavallo, p. 182.
247 La Legua came into being in 1947, following difficult negotiations between original inhabitants, the PCCh, and the government. Over the following 30 years, it experienced a rapid growth through construction of apartment buildings by ever more families that moved in – most of them at least sympathising communists.
248 Ibid, p 182.
249 Marío Garcés & Sebastián Leiva, p. 59.
250 Ascanio Cavallo, p. 219.
251 *Septiembre de 1973. Los cien combates de una batalla.*, (Gabriela Mistral, 1973), p. 26.
252 Ascanio Cavallo, p. 232.
253 Marío Garcés & Sebastián Leiva, p. 105.
254 Tanya Harmer, p. 184.
255 Ibid.
256 Ascanio Cavallo, p. 179.
257 Tanya Harmer, p. 186.
258 Max Marambio "La batalla en la embajada cubana el día del golpe", (*Diario La Tercera, Suplemento Reportajes*, 17 de agosto de 2003), cité in Ascanio Cavallo, pp. 177-178.
259 Ascanio Cavallo, p 243.
260 Tanya Harmer, p. 188.
261 Ascanio Cavallo, pp. 265-266.
262 Monica González, "Así fue como ocuparon la universidad",(*Revista Análisis*, 31 de marzo al 6 de abril de 1987)
263 Ascanio Cavallo, p. 264.
264 Christian Perez, 'Historia del Mir', pp 25-27
265 Tanya Harmer, p. 189.
266 Ascanio Cavallo, pp. 242-243.
267 Ascanio Cavallo, *La historia occulta del regimen militar*, (Uqbar Editores, 2008), pp. 53-57.
268 Ascanio Cavallo, *Golpe 11 de septiembre de 1973*, p. 268.
269 Ibid, p. 269.
270 John Dinges, p 57.
271 Franck Gaudichaud, p. 280.
272 Steve J. Stern, *Remembering Pinochet's Chile: On the Eve of London 1998*, (Duke University Press, 2009) pp. 180–81.
273 Franck Gaudichaud, p. 280.
274 Marie-Monique Robin, *Escadrons de la mort, l'école française*, (La Découverte, 2004), p. 287.
275 Sergio Zamora, *Histoire d'une trahison*, (Yvelinedition, 2013), pp. 134-135.
276 John Charles Chasteen, *Born in Blood and Fire: A Concise History of Latin America*, (W.W Norton and Company, 2001), p. 301.
277 Marie-Monique Robin, p 294.
278 Zamora, pp 159-163.
279 Ibid, p. 128.
280 Franck Gaudichaud, p. 281.
281 Cristián Pérez, 'Años de disparos y tortura (1973-1975): Los ultímos dias de Miquel Enríquez', (*Estudios Publicos*, spring 2004).
282 Christian Perez, 'Historia del MIR', p. 23.
283 Ibid, p. 21.
284 Ibid, p. 29.
285 Ibid, pp. 31-33.
286 Ibid, pp. 37-38.
287 Claudio Pérez Silva, 'El Frente Antifascista y la Politica Militar del Partido Comunista de Chile bajo dictatura, 1973-1980', (*Tempo e Argumento*, vol. 7, n° 16, september-december 2015), p. 172.
288 Juan Cristóbal Peña, *Los fusileros: Cronica secreta de une guerilla en Chile*, (Debate, 2007), p. 28.
289 Gazmuri, Jaime, *El Sol y la Bruma*, Antártica, 2000, p. 187.
290 Juan Cristóbal Peña, p. 30.
291 Ibid, p. 40.
292 Ascanio Cavallo, *La Historia secreta del regimen militar*, pp. 569-575.
293 Patricia Verdugo, Operación siglo XX. El atentado a Pinochet, (Editorial Catalonia, 2016).
294 Juan Cristóbal Peña, p. 207.
295 Ascanio Cavallo, *La Historia secreta del regimen militar*, p. 621.
296 Juan Cristóbal Peña, p.208.
297 Cristina Moyano Barahona, *El MAPU durante la dictatura*, (Ediciones Universitad Alberto Hurtado, 2010)
298 Bruno Patino: *Pinochet s'en va – La Transition démocratique au Chili (1988-1994)*, (IHEAL, 2000), pp. 87-89
299 Sergio Zamora, p. 204.
300 http://www.elmostrador.cl/noticias/pais/2017/11/19/muere-fernando-matthei-el-miembro-de-la-junta-militar-que-reconocio-el-triunfo-del-no-ante-la-presion-de-ee-uu/
301 Lefranc, Sandrine, *Politiques du pardon*, (Presses Universitaires de France, 2002) pp. 46-51.
302 Ibid, p. 43-44.
303 https://www.amnesty.be/infos/actualites/article/chili-la-mort-de-pinochet-n-arrete
304 'Les chefs d'accusation', *Courrier international*, no 416, 22 octobre 1998.
305 The lifting of General Pinochet's immunity is based on the fact that the amnesty law of 1978 applied to crimes, but not to the permanent offense of kidnapping which is then applied to the case of the disappeared.
306 General Juan Emilio Cheyre, "Ejército de Chile: el fin de una visión",(La Tercera, 11 May 2004).
307 'Las frases para el bronce de Pinochet', (*La Nacion*, 11 December 2006).
308 'Procesan a Pinochet y ordenan su arresto por los secuestros y homicidios de la "Caravana de la Muerte"', (*20minutos*, 28 November 2006).
309 'Las otras batallas por las calles de 11 septiembre', (*La Tercera*, 23 june 201)3.
310 http://www.derechoshumanos.udp.cl/derechoshumanos/images/InformeAnual/2015/INFORME%20COMPLETO%202015.pdf
311 Yasna Mussa, 'A 44 años del golpe de Pinochet, en Chile siguen luchando contra la impunidad' (New-York Times, 11 September 2017).

ACKNOWLEDGMENTS

I would like to express my gratitude for encouragement, support and help from my old friend Adrien Fontanellaz and Tom Cooper, without the help of whom I would not have been able to prepare this book. Albert Grandolini kindly shared plenty of original photography and information for this work, while Oscar Ruf Wilson helped sort out details about the FACh, and source additional photography.

Above all, I would like to devote this book to Sasha, my daughter, who patiently shared her daddy with a dark page of history: I can never thank her enough for her child's eyes full of innocence and love.

ABOUT THE AUTHOR

David François, from France, earned his PhD in Contemporary History at the University of Burgundy and specialised in studying militant communism, its military history and relationship between politics and violence in contemporary history. In 2009, he co-authored the *Guide des archives de l'Internationale communiste* published by the French National Archives and the Maison des sciences de l'Homme in Dijon. He is regularly contributing articles for various French military history magazines and the French history website L'autre côté de la colline. This is his first instalment for Helion.